ESMÉ CRAMPTON

Good Words, Well Spoken

A handbook of speech
for people in all walks of life

THE NORMAN PRESS
Toronto

By the same author
A HANDBOOK OF THE THEATRE

Canadian Cataloguing in Publication Data

Crampton, Esmé
  Good words, well spoken
  ISBN 0-9690375-0-3 pa.
  1. Voice.   2. Speech.   I. Title.
  PN4162.C72   808.5   C80-094664-2

The Norman Press
200 University Avenue
Suite 507
Toronto M5H 3C6

Contents

PART ONE: THE SOUNDING OF WORDS

Preface

The gift of speech is the mainspring of human communication. It affects every level of our lives, and is the primary source of the inheritance of language.

This is especially so now that we live in an age of instant communication. Technology has annihilated what used to be called the tyranny of distance. We can talk to virtually anyone on the phone, anywhere; interface with computers, telex messages; and see and hear the world via satellite, cable or lightwave television.

In turn, personal access and the availability of travel has opened an era of discussion by committee, of corporate decision, and of countless meetings, conferences, and seminars. In short, we are living in a new age of the oral tradition, and this, to some people, is an area for concern. Whereas it still takes work to prepare written reports, submissions, and briefs, it is frequently necessary to give oral reports, and to make and defend presentations as much through the spoken, as through the written, word. This need can apply whether we are connected with a school or college society, working in a business or a factory, in the professions or the arts, or helping a voluntary organization.

The spoken word is not only a means of conveying information, but a major means of establishing relationships, and a vital factor in creating a happy and fulfilling life. Aptly used, the spoken word can be a delight to listen to – trying to use it effectively is a continuing challenge throughout our lives.

To explore some of the ways of meeting this challenge, this book is divided into three major sections. Since it is important to understand the instrument through which we speak, the first covers *The Sounding of Words*. The second deals with those occasions when we need to say a few, or more, words in public and covers *Your Own Words*. The third section looks at the requirements of reading aloud and covers the use of *Other People's Words*.

Some readers will be more interested in certain chapters than in others, though everyone can stretch their potential by noting the content and trying the ideas in each one.

A feature of the book is a series of voice routines and assignments developed according to the content of each chapter. As an initial routine requires more background and preparation than others, it has been given a separate chapter. Each routine should be practised in sequence, and considered not as a series of things to be done, but as an experience to be developed. There is no one 'proper' way to speak, but these are among the techniques that can help build effectiveness. The real challenge lies in the gradual transition from new habit into daily use. This appears through the careful integration of the whole process, so that ideally we will mean as we sound, and sound as we mean.

As speech is a matter of interaction between people, it will help, if you are an individual reader, if you can find a friend or acquaintance who would also like to explore the development of the speaking voice, and to discover ideas for the use of words in action. Conversely, if you are a member of a class, and you can work in a large space, it will often be helpful to subdivide into small groups. In either case, a tape recorder will be useful.

Because communication of any kind cannot come from thin air, we will begin with an overview of the personal resources that provide the impulse that sets speaking and listening in motion. Then, like the house that Jack built, we will continue with many practical ideas so that you will gain personal insight and experience in using and in listening to good words, well spoken.

Acknowledgements

The author would like to thank the following for their kind permission to print the extracts included in this book: For three verses from *I Had A Hippotomus*, by Patrick Barrington, (©) 1933, Punch/Rothco, and for eight lines from *I Was A Bustlemaker Once, Girls*, by Patrick Barrington, (©) 1929, Punch/Rothco. For an extract from *Office Hours: Day And Night*, by Dr Janet Travell, The New American Library. For lines from *Under Milk Wood*, by Dylan Thomas, published by J.M. Dent And Sons, Ltd, the Trustees for the copyright of the late Dylan Thomas. For verses from *The Ballad Of The Mari Lwyd*, by Vernon Watkins, published by Faber And Faber, Ltd, Mrs Gwen Watkins. For an extract from *The Empty Space* published by Granada Publishing Limited, Mr Peter Brook. For an extract from an article in *Spoken English*, May 1974, published by the English Speaking Board (International) Mrs Christabel Burniston.

The author would like to acknowledge with thanks the help of Dr Steven Crainford and Professor Christine Rickards in reading the manuscript, and of Mr Patrick Drysdale for encouragement and interest.

GOOD WORDS, WELL SPOKEN

1
Introduction: Your Resources

It is generally agreed that what we say and how we say it are of equal importance. This handbook is designed to help you achieve your potential in both these areas.

It is equally important to recognize that what you say and how you say it are a compendium of all the 'yous' that ever you are and of all the 'hows' by which you express yourself. In other words, speech, like grooming or handwriting or any other aspect of human behaviour, is a manifestation of yourself and a true mirror of your personality.

The words that you speak and the way that you speak them are a vital factor in the conduct of your life, in the impression that others receive of you, and in the action that you may influence them to take. They are the often spontaneous, and sometimes carefully considered, result of your thoughts and feelings, and the medium by which you are the author and occasionally the poet of your particular dialogue with the world.

Since, as Martha Graham, the great American teacher of modern dance, once reminded her students, 'There is only one of you in all time,' we ought to consider a little who we are and how we express ourselves. And how the uttering, or what has been called the 'outering,' of the scheme of words called language fits within a total pattern of the marvel of the human ability to communicate.

First we should look at the essential qualities of our natural resources; and if that sounds like dealing in valuable oils and minerals, then it is useful to regard it in just that way. The following ingredients may be considered as the rock and root of the humanness of our being, which we use at different levels of experience throughout our interaction with life. Let us consider the first line of a whole communication tree (which appears in full on page 9), showing a range of means which enable us to communicate through speech.

SENDER

PERSONAL RESOURCES

Rhythm and co-ordination	Five special senses	Imagination	Emotion Thought	Voice
Movement and gesture	Common sense	Concentration	Intellect	Speech
Posture and relaxation	Intuitive sense		Experience Memory	

We are born with varying degrees of proficiency in our ability to use the above resources. For example, there is a *rhythm* in our lives from the moment we are born, when we are already capable of movement that is controlled by the inherent computer of our *co-ordination*. The result may be a general *movement*, which can involve the whole body in a fascinating exploration of space, or a particular movement of face or limb, so that already the range extends from facial expression to *gesture*. Through *relaxation* we are also born with the ability to let mind and muscle go, thus renewing energy and opening the channels of co-ordination to new impulses leading to further series of movements.

Next come the *five special senses* of sight, sound, smell, taste, and touch. These windows on the world enable us to receive impressions which, the more clearly they are perceived, in turn help us to understand and to share our experience with others. It is valuable to add to them that additional, or *common*, sense which governs an essential part of our daily living. It is also an important factor in any creative venture, often helping us to decide whether or not an idea will work in practice.

To the five special senses and common sense, many people like to add the less easy to define but intrinsic sense of *intuition*. This is that elemental source which is particularly true and often protective; which can be deeper and quicker than rational thought; and which can leap to the understanding to give insight or warning. (It is also part of that quick first impression on meeting people, which is a fascinating element in the building of relationships.)

Two further ingredients, which are often preceded by the words 'power of,' are those of *imagination* and *concentration*. Fundamentally they are interdependent, though the first may be regarded as an enormously vital resource, the second as an essential means by which all resources may be brought together, and which will receive continuous mention throughout the practical work in this book.

The imagination is a particularly intriguing quality since it is in one way the most abstract, and yet it lies at the root of all creative work and artistic expression. It can also be a hard one to explain and if, after you have thought about it, a definition seems elusive, it can help you to appreciate what imagination does if you consider what life would be like without it.

How would you bring images to mind, perceive the symbols that words represent, piece together bits of information, put memory to use, foresee consequences, and, even more important, be able to put yourself in somebody else's place? This of all qualities lies at the root of communicating with other human beings, which in turn often depends as much on the chemistry involved as on the actual work required to bridge many kinds of gaps. Imagination is also required for the dry runs or rehearsals for life which we call play and games, and is not only a human power but is available to an extent in the activities of some animals. Without it, life would surely be an expressionless desert, and a matter of one cement block staring at another cement block.

Back to the drawing-board, however, and perhaps to agreement that imagination is the ability to bring to mind and heart that which is not there at a given moment. Yet it becomes a power when the image carrying the impulse is so clear and strong that the very flavour of it, aided by the medium through which it is transmitted, creates a similar image in the mind and heart of someone else. So in the case of speech it is the joint medium of the words that you select to say and how you say them that transmits your stimulus into a response on the part of others.

In passing, it might be useful to mention that naturally the selection and arrangement of words also comes within the medium of the writer. But the interesting thing is that, while in some ways speaking and writing are similar – the one simply being a visual record, and some say a fossilized extension, of the other – in other ways they make different demands on their users. This is an important area of speech communication and will be pursued later, particularly in chapter 6.

The next qualities along the line to kindle speech are *emotion* and then *thought*. They are put in this order because we are born with the first and acquire the second, but tend to spend the latter part of our lives communicating more about the second than the first. Yet it is considered by many concerned people that if our expression of emotion and thought were more balanced, we would be able to identify and deal with average problems of both mental and physical health better than we do. Ability to express emotion can also have a contributing effect on the eventual development of the *intellect*, which uses knowledge with skill and originality, and can put *experience* and *memory* to positive use. Often easier to aim for than to achieve.

Finally, these resources are ready to be used at varying levels of need by the sound of the voice – made, as we shall find, by a series of movements which, like emotion, are instinctive; and by speech – again movement, but which, like thought, is acquired. Which brings us back to our initial point about what is said, or your words, always being balanced by how it is said, or your speaking voice.

This returns us to that encompassing resource of *concentration*, which provides that valuable sense of immersion within the recreation of experience, or within a topic, that at the same time allows some division of *awareness* for observation of the effect on others. This, in turn, brings us to the next generation of our communication tree.

VALUES: Expectation Attitude
KNOWLEDGE: Content Adaptability Delivery Awareness of Others
SPEECH TO INFORM INSTRUCT PERSUADE ENTERTAIN

One of the difficulties, as we shall discuss later, posed by the differences between the spoken and the written word is that, while in the case of both we need an *awareness* of the listener/reader, in the case of the spoken word we also need *adaptability*. In this sense the speaker has to be mercurially able to adapt to the twists and turns of the circumstances, dealing with the unexpected, with the new and with the old, while at the same time exercising the wisdom and restraint that are part of the pattern of effective listening. This is something the writer does not have to do; neither can he notice a grin or frown, be asked questions, or have to vary his pace. This is one of the reasons why some people used to the medium of the written word can be at odds with that of the spoken word, and find it difficult to adapt to a more personal activity.

A fundamental root of everyone's pattern of communication lies in personal values. For ultimately we communicate what we are, and what we are is a compound of what we believe. In short, effective communication depends upon integrity. Knowing how you feel and what you think about an issue is half the battle in expressing your views; but often we do not know our response until faced with the problem. Then comes the useful question, 'How do I know what I think – or feel – till I hear what I say?' Thus all forms of expression can be aids to discovery, and this is particularly applicable to the everyday form of speech.

In support of considering communication as involving what we are there comes the important matter of *expectation*, which tends to breed *attitude*. These factors can be the outcome of assumption and occasionally of prejudice – which we all have somewhere – and so they can have a special influence on what we say and how we say it. As far as possible it is helpful to avoid assumptions, as they not only clutter thinking but can sully relationships, sometimes doing so before these have a chance of being fairly established.

Next in line comes the sum total of our *knowledge* about the world, about others, and about ourselves, which may be both conscious and unconscious. Hopefully we can use the power of speech to share this resource with consideration for the views of others, and as a contribution rather than as a bludgeon. (This latter approach to communication will be discussed in a later chapter under the heading 'Making and receiving complaints.')

So much then for the range of many of the human qualities that are a continuing part of what we say and how we say it.

The next section of the family tree deals with *delivery*, and this aspect of how we speak is related to skills which will be discussed in the next four chapters and is closely dependent on the purpose of speaking. Apart from the private use of words in conversation, in family and ih social situations, public use is often described under the headings of speech to *inform, instruct, persuade*, and *entertain*.

Then comes a prolific generation of skills which are self-explanatory, and which can enable us to use our own, and interpret other people's, words as fully as possible. These help us to share, with all the completeness we can muster, the impulse behind what and how something is said.

SPEECH COMMUNICATION SKILLS

Physical	*Remedial*	*Aural*	*Intellectual*		*Public*		*Interpretive*
Relaxation	Sounds	Listening	Systems	Style	Public speaking		Reading aloud
Co-ordination	Accents	Ear-training	Codes	Feedback	Debate	Lecture	Prose
Breathing	Therapy		Signals	Loops	Committee	Sermon	Plays
Placing			Context		Discussion		Verse
Resonance					Demonstration		Choral speaking
					Interview		Acting
					Story-telling		
					Conversation		

Our communication tree now begins to fold the manner and content of speech back to the person, or groups of persons, for whom it is intended. The process can be accomplished by a wide variety of media, some involving an extension of the human ear (audio) and some the eye (video) and some an extension of both these members of our five special senses. And so, through whatever medium, speech carries over to the listener, whether he receives what we say and how we say it in private, in public, face-to-face, or face-to-electronic-media.

PERSON-TO-PERSON(S) MEDIA

Telephone	*P.A. Systems*	*Radio*	*Film*
Private	Airport	Am/Fm	8 mm
Party	Station	Network	16 mm
Conference	Hotel	Local	35 mm
Speakerphone	School	Open line	BW/Colour
Intercom	Factory	W/talkie	Stereoscopic
	Paging system		
Television	*Record*	*Theatre*	*Technology*
Network	Disc Cassette	Amplification	Computer
Local, Cable	Cartridge		Satellite
Closed circuit	Mono Stereo		Laser
BW/Colour	Audio Video		Hologram
Videophone	Answerphone		

Now comes the most important point of this section, and indeed perhaps of the whole book: *whatever you say and however you say it are, in turn, filtered through to the mind and heart of your listener by a similar – but not identical – set of personal resources and values and skills.*

RECEIVER: Individual Group Class Conference Congregation Audience

PERSONAL RESOURCES

Rhythm and co-ordination   Five special senses   Imagination   Emotion Thought   Voice

---

Within this multitude of potential for difference, which can colour even slight variations in the hearing and meaning given to words, is the miracle that we agree, share, agree to disagree, understand, and communicate at all with other human beings. So throughout your speaking life, aim to think of what you have to say not as an isolated event, but as a link in a chain in which you are often a craftsman and occasionally an artist – or, as the Greeks would have defined it, a joiner.

With the above considerations in mind, and with the chance of referring back to these common human denominators grouped on the next page within our total tree of communication, we turn to look at the development of your voice and speech in action.

SENDER

PERSONAL RESOURCES

Rhythm and co-ordination	Five special senses	Imagination	Emotion Thought	Voice
Movement and gesture	Common sense	Concentration	Intellect	Speech
Posture and relaxation	Intuitive sense		Experience Memory	

VALUES: Expectation Attitude

KNOWLEDGE: Content Adaptability Delivery Awareness of Others

SPEECH TO INFORM INSTRUCT PERSUADE ENTERTAIN

SPEECH COMMUNICATION SKILLS

Physical	Remedial	Aural	Intellectual		Public		Interpretive
Relaxation	Sounds	Listening	Systems	Style	Public speaking		Reading aloud
Co-ordination	Accents	Ear-training	Codes	Feedback	Debate	Lecture	Prose
Breathing	Therapy		Signals	Loops	Committee	Sermon	Plays
Placing			Context		Discussion		Verse
Resonance					Demonstration		Choral speaking
					Interview		Acting
					Story-telling		
					Conversation		

PERSON-TO-PERSON(S) MEDIA

Telephone	P.A. Systems	Radio	Film
Private	Airport	Am/Fm	8 mm
Party	Station	Network	16 mm
Conference	Hotel	Local	35 mm
Speakerphone	School	Open line	BW/Colour
Intercom	Factory	W/talkie	Stereoscopic
	Paging system		

Television	Record	Theatre	Technology
Network	Disc Cassette	Amplification	Computer
Local, Cable	Cartridge		Satellite
Closed circuit	Mono Stereo		Laser
BW/Colour	Audio Video		Hologram
Videophone	Answerphone		

RECEIVER: Individual Group Class Conference Congregation Audience

PERSONAL RESOURCES

Rhythm and co-ordination	Five special senses	Imagination	Emotion Thought	Voice

Part One
The Sounding of Words

2
Your Voice

Few people realize that the speaking voice is a musical instrument; or that in terms of physics it has three components which produce a sound. They are: an excitor, or force, which provides power; a vibrator, which when set in motion makes the sound; and a resonator which re-sounds, or amplifies, the result.

In the piano, for example, the excitor is the force of the finger striking the keys; in the violin, it is the bow against the strings. In the case of both, the vibrator is the string which is set in motion. The resonator is the hollow case where the vibrations are amplified and given a characteristic quality, according to the shape and material of which it is composed. (Fig. 1)

The excitor in your speaking voice, as you will have guessed, is the breath; the vibrator is formed by your vocal cords. They provide the sound which is amplified into tone by the three-part sound-box of your resonator, which is created by the adaptive use of your throat, mouth, and nose. So a musical note is produced, and so the basic training in speaking and singing is similar; they are branches of the same tree, the roots of their development being identical.

Here it is helpful to remember that there is a difference between the sounds we shall hopefully make, and what is known as noise. In sound the vibrations are regular and follow a rhythmic pattern; in noise the vibrations are irregular in recurrence, and are decidedly harsh and unpleasing to the ear. (Fig. 2)

Meanwhile our own instrument possesses another factor which, in comparison with any other musical instrument, gives us an extra dimension. We can not only transmit breath into a musical sound and enlarge it in our joint resonator to produce tone; we can also mould the tone, and even interrupt it by the action of tongue and lips, so forming the sounds of speech, which

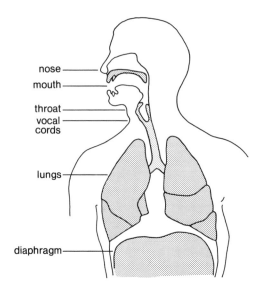

Figure 1 Relationship of the components of the voice

together make words. We have therefore both a tone-producing and a word-producing instrument.

To appreciate that your voice is dependent on your breath, try a simple experiment:

1 Breathe right out.
2 Try to say 'hullo, hullo, hullo.'

If you really followed (1) it is unlikely that you could produce any voice at all for the third 'hullo.' Now you know what it is like consciously to be without breath – resolve never to be in the same boat again, and to take special note of the breathing exercises to come.

sound

noise

Figure 2 Oscillograph

Breath – the power behind the throne

So the speaker requires breath, breath, and more breath. Without the medium of force there can be no vibration, since the vocal cords could not be set in motion; and there can be no sure placing of tone or maintenance of pitch. Consequently the voice would lack control and any amount of concentration or other effort would have a hit-or-miss result. Remember that breath is to the speaker what touch is to the pianist, wind to the flautist, or bags of air to the bagpiper. So one of the first aims in developing the voice is to work towards an eventual sense of control of this motive power. It will take perseverance and, since initial improvement is often the most difficult hurdle to cross, is dependent on trust. The process is similar to going on a diet – be thorough about the basics, gradually discover your own needs, and be sure to keep in regular practice.

To discover where, when, and how to adapt the everyday action of breathing for the purpose of speech, our next concern is with the structure of the rib-cage, which was created for the primary function of protecting heart and lungs.

THE RIB-CAGE

We have twelve pairs of ribs, which are all attached to the spine at the back. In front, only the first seven pairs are attached, and these to the sternum, or breastbone; the next three pairs are the longest and are attached indirectly to the sternum by cartilage. The last two pairs are unattached in front; depending on any padding we may have in the area, not all of us can feel them, but they are known under the optimistic title of the false, or floating, ribs.

Since the upper seven pairs are attached back and front, there will be comparatively limited movement in this area. But considerable all round movement is possible in the area of the eighth to the tenth ribs. Here, when the shoulders are relaxed, the posture is good, and there is no unnecessary tension, the beginner may discover an expansion of five to eight centimetres. To check:

1 Breathe right out, without strain, while holding a tape measure lightly round the area.
2 Breathe in, easily, and you will have to let the tape slide out by so many centimetres.

Try the same after two or three months and, the muscles having become more limber, or flexible, the cage will probably expand by another two or three centimetres or so – the maximum being up to about eleven centimetres. This important action will allow for greater capacity of breath, a surer development of tone, and later for a better control of meaning through phrasing.

The muscles which raise the ribs in what is often described as a bucket-handle movement – which also brings the base of the sternum slightly forward and up – are the two sets of intercostal, or between-rib, muscles. These are the interior and exterior intercostals, and they create a spreading action through a structure rather like the webbing on a duck's foot.

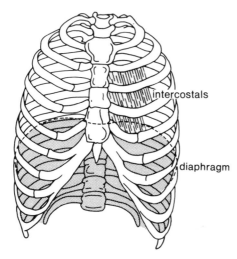

Figure 3 Rib-cage from the front, indicating muscles

The intercostals, therefore, are the muscles we exercise to increase the expansion of this heavy, protective cage; and this is the movement which creates a vacuum which causes the sponge-like lungs to take in oxygen. The expansion of the cage is three-way: first, side-to-side, coupled with front-to-back, both caused by the intercostals; and top-to-bottom, caused by the action of a further muscle called the diaphragm.

The diaphragm is a large muscle which we can neither feel nor touch. Forming the floor of the chest and the roof of the abdomen, it is similar to a tilted mushroom; the lower sides of the dome are attached to the periphery of the lower ribs. Its fibres converge towards a large central tendon, which, like the stalk of our mushroom, slants down and back towards insertion at the lumbar vertebrae. As you breathe in, and as the rib-cage expands outwards, the diaphragm contracts, flattening the large dome and so enlarging the cavity of the chest from top to bottom.

Mention should be made here that the term contraction in the above sense does not imply tension. As you will remember, muscles run in pairs, and it takes a minimum of two to complete any movement. As one contracts, providing the initial motive power, the other relaxes, allowing the movement to take place. The reverse then occurs, as the first muscle relaxes and the second contracts, completing the swing of the movement. This swing, for example, is what happens between the two sets of rib muscles every time you breathe in and out. (Incidentally, it is a cheerful thought that because breathing is a reflex action it is impossible to commit suicide by holding the breath.) Anyway, you will find that an initial important breathing exercise is called 'rib-swing' and should be faithfully practised every single day.

Meanwhile, as the dome of the diaphragm contracts and flattens, a further ingenious movement takes place. If you put a hand lightly on that space below the sternum where the rib-cage divides, and if you then take an easy breath, you will feel a slight protrusion. This bulge is caused by a displacement of organs, such as the liver; and if there were not space for this to happen, you would feel an uncomfortable sense of pressure every time the dome descended. The splendid name given to this front muscular space, sometimes mistaken for the diaphragm, is the epigastrium.

It is worth remembering that while, if you are relaxed, there may be this slight protrusion in the space above the waist during an intake of breath, there is no need for any excess movement below. Since this is unnecessary for the vital purpose of breathing, which is to oxygenate the blood, it is unnecessary for the secondary purpose of speech. Were the whole abdominal wall to be brought into action, a large tummy could easily develop. Whereas an effective approach to breathing will not make for increase in any padding and should, with consistent practice of the exercises, help firm it away.

Voice – the vibrator

A brief outline of the structure of the larynx, or voice-box, will be useful for occasional reference later, but once the main workings are understood, the details can be stored away. We cannot feel the muscles that make the sound of the voice, although we have some sensation of the result; and although they come under voluntary control, that control is indirect, being maintained by our hearing and the pressure of our breath. The following can give an appreciation of the miracle and complexity of the mechanism; it can also given an insight into what we do, albeit unconsciously, when we speak; and into what we hear others do when they speak.

THE LARYNX

The larynx is composed of cartilage (the same material used for the end of the nose and the edge of the ears) which is formed into a three-part, protective box. The base is composed of a ring which is virtually the topmost ring of the windpipe, or trachea. Balanced on the top and back of this ring, or cricoid cartilage, are the two smaller arytenoid cartilages, capable of swivelling their triangular bases towards, or away from, the centre. Surrounding and protecting these arytenoids at front and sides is the more familiar thyroid cartilage; this is shaped rather like two wings, with a promontory at their join in front, otherwise known as the Adam's apple. Stretching from just inside this promontory, and attached to the front processes of these little arytenoid cartilages, are the vocal cords.

Their inner edges are free; and normally, when at rest, there is a gap between them, known as the glottis, through which breath passes in and out soundlessly. But when we wish to use the voice, the intricate co-ordination of mind and tiny muscle causes the front process of the arytenoids to swivel, almost closing the glottis. The cords are now like two lips approximated, or just barely touching.

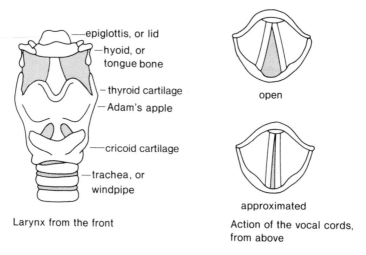

epiglottis, or lid
hyoid, or tongue bone
thyroid cartilage
Adam's apple
cricoid cartilage
trachea, or windpipe

Larynx from the front

open

approximated

Action of the vocal cords, from above

Figure 4　The larynx

The closing of the glottis is timed to occur with the onset of the breath which, rushing between the free inner edges of the cords, sets up a vibration, causing the particular sound we know as voice. This vibrating column of air is reinforced in the lower resonator of the throat, and then moulded into speech as it continues up and out through the major cavities of the mouth and nose.

PITCH AND RANGE OF THE VOICE
Pitch, or height and depth of the voice, is determined by two main factors:

1 The number of times at which the vocal cords vibrate per second.
2 Our natural range, which is dependent on the length and thickness of the cords.

The frequency of vibration is dependent not only on the force of the breath, but also on the particular adjustments that have been made in the larynx. The listener hears this as the pitch of the voice.

So if we wish to sustain a pitch, we must have sufficient force, or breath. But if the force diminishes, the pitch, like an old, unwinding record player, will drop, gradually accompanied by a similar fade in volume. This, incidentally, is the cause of a problem in some inexperienced speakers who can be heard at the beginning of a paragraph or phrase but appear to have a habit of fading away at the end.

Our range of pitch is determined by the length, thickness, and changing degree of pull, or slight tension exerted on the cords. Again as with other musical instruments, so with us. The longer and thicker the string, the lower the note; hence the difference between the higher notes of the strings of a violin, and the lower notes of those of a double bass. Those of us who have longer, thicker cords will have naturally lower voices than those with shorter, thinner cords, though the actual physical difference in length can be very slight. It is estimated that the vocal cords of a man are approximately two centimetres long, and of a woman, one-and-a-quarter centimetres, with a proportionate difference in the size of the resonator.

Our natural pitch is changed by the degree of tension of the cords, rather as the note on a violin is changed when it is being tuned, when tightening or slackening of the string produces a higher or lower result. But where most musical instruments have at least five, and often more, strings to produce a full range, we have only two, which needless to say can never be replaced. Ideally, the small muscles inside the larynx exert this changing pull to reflect our mood and meaning, and the rise and fall is unconscious and automatic, though as previously mentioned it is controlled by the ear. This is why people who are affected by some degree of deafness may have somewhat unchanging voices.

Should there be a marked degree of unnecessary tension in the body as a whole, and in particular in the area of the head, back, and shoulders, this can be reflected in unnecessary tension in the voice. Any tightening of muscles in the area could lead to some lack of voice control, a higher pitch than necessary, and a thinning of the sound through probable constriction of the resonator.

So the degree to which we are strained, or nervous, is likely to be reflected in the voice, though careful practice of the exercises will help keep the instrument free. The opposite can hold when health is out of sorts and we are depressed and lack vitality. The energy to breathe well is lacking; the voice, when the condition is serious, lacks power and has a limited range, residing mostly around the lower notes.

The speaking voice is concerned with a range of about five pitches, or notes, rather than the wide range of sixteen or more notes of the singing voice. But five to ten minutes a day of singing scales, for those who feel inclined, is an excellent exercise for every speaker; the process helps awaken the ear to a wide range of pitch, and helps lubricate, as it were, all the muscles concerned with breath and voice. But there would be little value in passing results of even perfect pitch through a poorly shaped resonator, so it is time to look into the matter of tone.

Tone

First it may be helpful to define tone in our sense as a quality of voice, rather than implying mood, as in the familiar phrase, 'tone of voice.'

The development of tone in the speaking voice is dependent on the third component present in all instruments which produce a musical sound: the resonator. This, you will remember, is generally a cavity through which the vibrations of the strings of the violin, the parchment of the drum, or of our vocal cords are amplified.

Just as in the previous chapter, in order to appreciate the power of imagination, we considered what life would be like without it, so it is enlightening to consider sound without this amplification. Imagine a violin with strings, bridge and adjustments, but without the box underneath. Think of plucking or bowing one of the strings, and the result would be recognizable in pitch, but decidedly small and thin in quality. The same would apply to the piano if you took away the case which surrounds the mechanism of keys, hammers and strings. Think of striking some notes, and even of playing a familiar tune. Again you would recognize the result, though the quality would be as different from the usual as skimmed milk is from cream. So it would be with the speaking voice if, by chance, the vibrations passed straight into the air, without going through the joint cavity of our resonator. Proper use of this space is a major factor in developing a good speaking voice.

PRINCIPLES OF RESONANCE
To understand the function of our resonator, we turn to the subject of physics. We find that if we disturb the air, or set up a vibration within any cavity by blowing across its opening, or by blowing through any openings, we hear a note of a definite pitch. Try blowing across the top of an empty bottle. The result is known as resonant pitch and is an inherent factor within any hollow cavity. The height or depth of this pitch is determined by the size of the hollow, and by the number and size of its openings. A large resonator will give a low pitch; and a small resonator, a high pitch. Consider the difference, for example, in blowing across a small bottle and a large one. So it is that, while all voices have a potential resonance, some will have a fuller quality than others, depending on physique.

The number and size of the openings also influence this resonant pitch. To illustrate this, take another simple resonator, such as an empty matchbox. Hold it lightly and, with the lid closed, tap it; you will hear a note of a certain pitch. Open it a bit, tap it again, and the pitch will rise. Open it still further, and the pitch will rise again. Repeat the process with a larger box and, as with the bottles, the resultant pitch will be lower than with the smaller one.

If you wished to take the process a step further you could bore holes in a resonator and cover them with your fingers. As you took your fingers off the holes and the number of openings increased, so the pitch would rise again. This is what occurs in a reed instrument, such as a flute or oboe, when the vibration of the reed remains constant and the pitch is changed by the openings in the resonator.

We are, however, a stringed and a wind instrument and, as we know, our pitch is fundamentally changed by the frequency of the vibration of our vocal cords. But because of our series of cavities, or openings, above the cords, we also possess this quality of resonant pitch; and it is this which continually reinforces our vocal pitch. Without it, the voice would have that quality of skimmed milk rather than of cream, and the result would be thin and reedy. So, reinforced by good posture, we need to develop the full potential amplification of our sound. This reduces unnecessary effort, provides efficient use of breath, and aids eventual projection through the 'ring' imparted by the harmonics of good resonance.

These are among the reasons why it is vitally important that the individual voice is not forced by misleading advice towards a higher or lower range than that of which it is naturally capable. In a later section of exercises, we shall discuss how the natural range of a voice may be assessed.

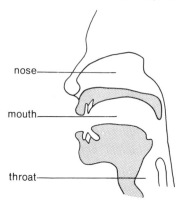

nose—

mouth—

throat—

Figure 5 Joint resonator of the voice

The throat is the first cavity in which the vibrations of the voice are amplified. Known as the pharynx, it is like a hollow toothpaste tube stretching up the back of the mouth to the back of the nose. As we know, it is vitally important that this whole area of the neck is well held; physical imbalance or inner tension can constrict the muscles, hardening the walls of the tube and resulting in a harsh and unfortunate quality in the voice.

The oral cavity of the mouth is spherical in shape, and is the most mobile part of our resonator. The size, shape, and openings being changed by the lower jaw, lips, tongue, and soft palate. These acquired movements mould our column of sound into speech. An effective routine will include exercises for control and co-ordination of these muscles; a stiff jaw, or lips, for example, can impair the resonance, keeping the mouth and openings permanently small. It will also be helpful to learn to keep the tip of the tongue flat and out of the way for sounds, such as vowel sounds, for which it does not need to be raised. It often comes as a surprise that the tongue muscle is as large as it is, for it originates in the hyoid bone, just above the larynx. It is also very powerful, and yet capable of subtle varieties of movement. Among other things it is largely responsible for the pronunciation of, at a conservative estimate, the over 3,000 languages and the multitude of their dialects and accents spoken by man.

If you now feel the roof of your mouth with the tip of the tongue, you will touch many points with which contact is made to articulate some of the sounds of speech. First, starting from the front, there is the back of the upper teeth where 'th' is made. A little higher, and on a ridge, comes the place for 't,' and just behind that, the place for 'n'; then you will feel the hard palate, where the tongue curls for some 'r' sounds. The palate also provides a useful sounding-board for the voice, helping to conduct vibrations out through the mouth and towards other cavities. Some resonance is obtained in the frontal sinuses just over the eyes, for example. Then at the very back of the mouth the roof becomes soft and fleshy, and is used for the sounds 'g' and 'k.'

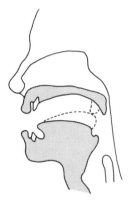

Figure 6 Action of the soft palate,
as for 'ng' followed by 'AH'

The soft palate acts as a form of valve which, when raised, shuts off the passage from the mouth into the nose; this happens for all but three sounds of English. The three sounds for which the palate is lowered are known as the nasal consonants and are 'm,' 'n,' and 'ng.' Should the palate be lazy, however, it tends to stay lowered, particularly when under the influence of one of these sounds in a word. The result is what is known as nasal tone, which is unfortunate, producing a particular form of twang in the voice. An extreme form occurs when occasionally the palate is affected by paralysis, or when a child is born with the condition called a cleft palate. Then air escapes continuously into the nose, colouring all sounds. Fortunately the operation to join this cleft is now considered very simple, and with effective speech therapy lasting effects are rare.

The third part of our resonator, the nose, is a triangular-shaped cavity which is divided by a small central bone called the septum. You will soon discover that, although it is not capable of movement, it makes an important contribution to the general quality of voice. We have already discussed nasal tone, which occurs when this cavity is overused. To discover what it is like when under used, try holding the nose, as if you had a first-class cold, and the result is muffled and dead.

The aim throughout is to achieve a balanced use of all three resonators. Too much in the throat, for example, and the result is heavy, strangled, and later difficult to project; too much in the mouth, and the voice sounds as if it lacks foundation. The best way to achieve this balance is by projecting the channel of sound forwards, towards the listener, and through the mask, or front, of the face. By maintaining a good alignment of the head, neck, and spine, keeping up the pressure of breath from below and aiming to fill all cavities with the sound on its way out, all channels are open for the production of a good, resonant voice.

3
A Voice Routine

Now it is time for a look at the practical work suggested in this book. Regular practice of a voice routine is essential, and a developing core of exercises follows each chapter in part I. In parts II and III you will also find assignments designed to give experience in adapting to various topics. They will include a wide variety of situations, ranging from the glad to the sad, the sublime to the ridiculous, and, often hardest, the everyday to the ordinary.

The concept of a routine depends on regular practice, but is not intended to denote a fixed, precise outline; although initially, as in going on a diet, it is important to become familiar with the essentials. Then develop your own repertoire of, for example, material for reading aloud, and of ideas for assignments. Always start, however, with the ritual of the routine for, in addition to tuning your voice, it is a valuable means of bringing together the resources of inner discipline that are required in any effective form of communication.

USE OF A TAPE RECORDER
For those interested in monitoring progress, it can be helpful to make judicious use of a tape-recorder, but this should be tempered in the light of the human element involved. For example, while an initial control recording can be made, further tapings should not be expected to show any development for some months – as what mind and heart can understand takes time for muscle to digest. Making too many early comparisons would be like the actions of two children who dug up their plants each day to see if the roots were growing....

Be prepared to set aside the control recording for three to six months, and use another tape, which you can keep erasing as you go, for everyday work. This will be similar to a rough book, or series of working notes, as used by artists or craftsmen in many fields before committing final work to their appropriate medium. But you may like to add a record of more finished achievements to the other side of your control tape.

Making a tape
If you are inexperienced in making a tape, the following points can help in saving you time and repeat recordings:
- Double-check any manual for the tape-recorder, and rehearse the use of controls.
- Unless built in, keep the microphone as far away from the machine as you can; otherwise the whirr of moving parts will act on the tape as a slight barrier to your voice.
- Microphones vary in sensitivity, so pre-test for the volume you need, and check the tone control.
- For best reproduction, speak within about sixty centimetres of the mike, and use the automatic volume control where available.
- Where a counter is available, set it to zero before starting a new tape, and always note the number at which you finish. List this, and the contents of each (even brief) recording, on the tape itself and, if possible, on the outside of any cartridge, cover, or box. Never leave a tape unidentified.
- On most machines there is a slight delay before the tape picks up the recording; let it run for about five seconds before speaking. To re-record, simply rewind and use the microphone as before; the new recording will automatically erase the old.

Control tape
Take your time. Choose four from the following seven items, and have your material ready. Let the recording run during each item, though you may need to turn it off between items. First, give your name and the date.

1 With brief preparation, such as a once-over for content, but without rehearsal as such, read aloud the following prose passage:

It was the best of times, it was the worst of times, it was the age of wisdom, it was the age of foolishness, it was the epoch of belief, it was the epoch of incredulity, it was the season of Light, it was the season of Darkness, it was the spring of hope, it was the winter of despair, we had everything before us, we had nothing before us, we were all going direct to Heaven, we were all going direct the other way – in short, the period was so far like the present period, that some of its noisiest authorities insisted on its being received, for good or for evil, in the superlative degree of comparison only.

There were a king with a large jaw and a queen with a plain face, on the throne of England; there were a king with a large jaw and a queen with a fair face, on the throne of France. In both countries it was clearer than crystal to the lords of the State preserves of loaves and fishes, that things in general were settled for ever.

It was the year of Our Lord one thousand and seven hundred and seventy-five. Spiritual revelations were conceded to England at that favoured period, as at this. Mrs Southcott had recently attained her five-and-twentieth blessed birthday, of whom a prophetic private in the Life Guards had heralded the sublime appearance by announcing that arrangements were made for the swallowing up of London and Westminster. Even the Cock-lane ghost had been laid only a round dozen of years, after rapping out its messages, as the spirits of this very year last past (supernaturally deficient in originality) rapped out theirs. Mere messages in the earthly order of events had lately come to the English Crown and People, from a congress of British subjects in America; which, strange to relate, have proved more important to the human race than any communications yet received through any of the chickens of the Cock-lane brood.

From *A Tale of Two Cities* by Charles Dickens

2 Read aloud without rehearsal a passage of your own choice, of about the same length, but including some dialogue.
3 Read aloud a passage of your own writing such as part of a report of a meeting, or account of a sports event, a play, or a concert you have enjoyed.
4 Read a short scene from a play, either concentrating on a whole speech, or taking many parts; or read aloud a few verses from a favourite poem.
5 In your own words, but using notes to jog the memory if necessary, give a three-minute account of someone you have met recently who has impressed you – perhaps during an interview, at work, or at school or college. Try to make the person as vivid as you can, as if you are actually talking, but talking well, to a listener.
6 In your own words, give a five-minute account of some memorable experience, making it as vivid as possible for your listener.
7 Do a five-minute interview, as for radio, of a friend, about one unique thing about him or her – volunteer work, an unusual hobby or interest, or something he or she has helped start, such as a magazine or club or society. Likewise, ask a friend to interview you.

Apart from a quick check to see that the recording took, put it aside for about six months.

AIMS OF YOUR VOICE ROUTINE

Because some of the following exercises can appear deceptively simple, it is important to view them with an understanding of their aims. If the voice is to become free and flexible, and because it is interconnected with our systems of breathing, posture, and general mental and physical co-ordination, it needs to live in an equally flexible physique. So a voice routine best begins with a few minutes' relaxation lying on the floor, not with the aim of becoming a sack of potatoes, but to encourage a sensation of muscular ease. Then, working from general to particular areas, the memory of this sensation can be transferred to the movement of breathing, which activates the sound of the voice. Similarly, as work progresses to an individual sound, such as the hum, and as this becomes more forward and resonant, the memory of a positive sensation can be applied to further sounds, and so into words and on into whole phrases of speech.

Meanwhile nothing very tangible can be expected to happen for a few weeks, since there may be a period of change from usual habits and attitudes. If development is to be true to the personality and physique, adaptation of the speaking instrument is likely to be gradual. But improvement can become noticeable in various ways, including a reserve of power because of more open breathing, an almost imperceptible change in posture, and a fuller sense of resonance and development of confidence. The changes are at one level simple, but because of the interrelationships they are also complex, and are unlikely to be quickly evident to other people.

The fact that they are not obvious can be a form of accolade, for it is usually a sign that development comes from inside the personality and understanding. Such development can gradually be accompanied by fewer requests to speak up, or to repeat phrases, and so in some cases lead to a sense of vocal participation in life not perhaps previously experienced.

Yet practice of the spoken word should not be regarded as a remedial form of study and be given time only because 'something is wrong.' Therapy of many kinds can make an invaluable contribution to those with special needs, but most people can afford to give the same attention to communicating through the spoken word as they do to the written word. Not only is it just as possible to develop the gift of speech, but it is now becoming vital that we do so. The speed at which technological change is enabling us to communicate is also taking us into a new era of the oral tradition.

So a voice routine, initially lasting ten to fifteen minutes, should be practised at least three or four times a week. It should be preceded by a time of
preparation, include relaxation and consideration of posture, and continue
into exercises which will work towards a gradual transition of new habits into
everyday life.

PREPARATION
- Find a quiet spot, ease any neckwear and take off shoes.
- Because it is important that the neck is free, let your head go first. Then
  kneel on your hands and knees, roll over to one side, and so on your
  back, and lie on the floor.
- Take a few moments to forget past cares; let yourself breathe easily and
  deeply three or four times.
- With feet apart, bend the knees and hitch the pelvis up off the floor
  about thirty centimetres, so that without going to the length of standing
  on your head the blood can circulate in the opposite direction for a
  minute.
- Let the pelvis down, and let the knees be so relaxed that the legs
  straighten and the feet fall to the sides.
- Roll the head from side to side easily and vigorously, without strain;
  think of all your muscles and joints as being as flexible and open as possible.
- With the head still, let the feet flop in and out just as easily.
- Let yourself breathe slowly and deeply three or four times.

Relaxation
Build on your own ideas to let you relax physically and mentally. These can
include a letting-go of all muscles, naming areas through the head-face-neck,
and on down through the shoulders, arms, and hands, and so through the
trunk, legs, feet, and toes. Another idea is to visualize the muscles and check
their let-go as if you had a small flashlight within. Using, if you wish, a form
of mantra, check the following points:

spine lengthen, neck free;
back widen, shoulders open.

The aim is to release unnecessary tension which, if it exists in one part of
the body, can easily be transferred to the voice. A prime result of tension is
the often unconscious prevention of ease of movement; for most people
have a tendency to protect themselves from, or to compensate for, aspects of

life that create pressure. Such a tendency, whether caused by humping a heavy briefcase or by sitting in a slouch, can become a habit. So it is helpful to precede any voice work with a period of calm, of lengthening of the spine, and of opening awareness to the harmony of the whole.

To help you relax mentally, let your mind take you somewhere with pleasant associations. Close your eyes and focus on the sights, sounds, and smells or what-have-you of a favourite or ideal vacation spot. Even such a three- to five-minute break from the previous round of the day can refresh and replenish energy.

– Slowly open your eyes and let your breathing muscles work easily and deeply, from the bottom of the chest to the top, five or six times. And if you find yourself yawning, all the better.

You are now ready to make an easy, free-flowing sound. Pause and, with your inner ear, be ready to listen for the sensation of a voiced sigh, as in 'H-AH.'

– Take a deep, wide breath through the nose and, without holding it, let the return-swing of the ribs activate the voice.
– Let it feel as if the sound is part of a direct line of sensation from your toes through your trunk, neck, and mouth, and on up to the ceiling.
– Repeat the voiced sigh on a falling, and on a steady, note.
– Pause and repeat both a few more times, now letting each become as full of voice as possible rather than resembling any kind of half-whisper.
– Roll the head gently from side to side to check that the neck remains easy, and do some more deep, wide breathing.
– Without hurry, or trying to attain results other than ease of sensation, repeat this open, voiced sound. The aim is simply to become aware of how your voice feels when it is working under free conditions, without mental or physical constraint.

By gradually building in a consistent memory of such ease of use, you can discover how well your voice can work if, as in the case of other uses of muscular energy, you think the process through and let it happen, rather than straining for results. The next stage will be to carry the same sensation into using the voice while standing, and then sitting or moving, according to need. For everyone can make best use of the voice when all the systems involved work openly and in harmony; and such principles provide effective roots whether they will eventually be needed by public speaker, teacher, actor, preacher, or home-maker.

Standing
Before standing, take a minute to pre-think the movement involved so that, rather than inadvertently setting up habits that can impede, you carry a remembered sense of ease with you. Let your head stay down until last, so that your neck can remain free, and your spine will gradually uncurl in one flowing movement.

- Slowly roll over sideways, come up on to your knees and, using your hands to help, begin to stand.
- Think of wearing your head well, as a continuation of the spine.
- Keep the weight of the body slightly forward, more on your toes than on your heels.
- Think of your scalp as being roughly parallel to, and lifting the body towards, the ceiling.

Posture
The way we move and hold ourselves affects the way we use the voice. Because of the need for a good alignment of the head, neck, and spine, and since it is astonishingly easy to develop unfortunate slouches and slumps, here is an idea which can be helpful to remember.

- Think of having an imaginary hook just behind the centre of your scalp; wherever you stand, sit or move, this attaches you to the ceiling by a strong piece of elastic, which is an extension of the elasticity of the spine.

This leads to two advantages for the voice: a good balance of the head helps efficient use of muscles in the neck and shoulder area; the sense of stretching and lengthening of the spine can lead to a valuable expansion of the lower back area of the rib-cage, leading to a natural increase of power and control of the voice.

- Think of the spine as a necklace dangled above a surface. Compare this to a necklace lowered and curved by the pressure of the surface on which it rests. Then imagine the twelve pairs of ribs opening, diagram-matically, at right angles to the spine; and you gain some idea of the difference between breathing as from within a longer and more open column, compared to breathing as from within a column that is compressed and curved.

From now on, slouching is a no-no.

Sitting and standing
Since posture is concerned with a balanced use of the body in action and in repose, two of our everyday actions need a check.

- When sitting and standing, think of using the pelvis rather than the waist as a joint.
- Maintain the idea of lengthening the spine, but carry the head at right angles to it, and let it give a sense of lift to the action.
- Avoid any sense of leading with the chin, which can create a pattern of tilting the head back, so compressing the spine and allowing the shoulders to tilt and droop.
- When either movement is complete, make it a habit to remind yourself about that piece of elastic which connects you to the ceiling.

Walking
- Maintain a sense of elasticity.
- Before moving off, it is helpful to find a sense of propulsion as from the top of the head, by inserting a small loose-leaf notebook, about two centimetres thick, under the heels as a slight wedge. Try to remember the resultant sense of forward balance and lift, and see if you can use it to make walking light and easy.

Infinitesimal as these points may seem, they should be considered as an intrinsic part of your routine, for a good pattern of general use of the body will enable you to set up a good pattern for the voice.

EXERCISES
- Carry the sensation of ease into standing.
- Keep the feet a little apart, the weight forward, and the shoulders relaxed and down.
- Check that the neck is relaxed by gently rotating the head, or letting it fall from side to side, or front to back. Always finish in a good resting, or balanced, position.

– Take three or four easy breaths through the nose; each time letting the ribs work in one complete swinging movement. Never take in a breath and hold it; such an action cannot make sound, which depends on the return-swing of the outgoing air.

If you think of the above as a rib-swing exercise, you have a reminder that just as a golfer practises the continuity of his stroke, so you should always consider the action of breathing as one movement and not two separate movements.

First open sound
– Maintain an easy posture.
– Keep the weight forward.
– Let the lower jaw grow heavy, and the mouth drop open.

This opening should be big enough to allow the top joint of the thumb to be placed in the mouth vertically. At the same time the tip of your tongue should touch your lower front teeth, and the rest of the tongue should lie flat and relaxed, so keeping it out of the way when not needed. Ideally the tongue descends with the jaw, like the floor of an elevator. But don't worry that this is going to make you look strange when finally in business. It is simply to help you retain that sense of 'all channels open' so that you are ready for that now familiar, voiced sigh.

– Take three or four easy breaths, letting each out through this completely open sound.
– Pause a minute, check general ease, particularly the elasticity of the head and neck area, and repeat your voiced sigh.
– Think of gently leaning the forward weight of the body behind the voice. If you briefly resemble the tower of Pisa, no matter, as it will help the outgoingness of the sound, and mentally and physically help pre-set the major needs of projection.

Soon you can relax the jaw even more, so that it will open to the combined width of the second and middle fingers popped in and out vertically. Otherwise all the opening of your throat, and intended ease elsewhere, will be negated. For as you will find in the following chapter, it is essential that the circumference of the final opening or megaphone of your voice is flexible if the sound is to be effectively channelled. And while this may be common sense in theory, it is surprising how initially people find it hard to remember in practice. Think of it as an extension of the usual movement of the jaw, for it does not imply you will be expected to mouth words or produce the artificialities of the 'how-now-brown-cow' syndrome. The slight stretching involved in exercising the jaw more than you usually do gives a greater ease and control later.

A useful check for an open throat, relaxed jaw, and flat tongue can be made by looking in a mirror. For it is worth remembering that a good sound is controlled both by the ear and by the shaping of the cavities through which the sound passes.

– Position the mirror in a good light so that you can look into the arch of the throat, and avoid any tilting of the head. If you are doubtful about the openness of the arch, breathe easily a few times, and look again during a yawn. Then without strain let the jaw drop and see if the back of the roof of the mouth is as raised as the tongue is flat.

Should the arch usually seem considerably lower than when you yawn you may have the all too frequent habit of a lazy soft palate; and it is important to work on this as it can lead to a nasal tone. This is caused by a proportion of the sound escaping up and behind the droop and so out through the nose. But a relaxed concentration, as mind on matter, can begin to alleviate the pattern.

Gradually the new muscular memory of the open sensation of neck and throat can be carried into the everyday use of your voice. And as we shall find in the extension of your routine following the next chapter, it can help combine a first sense of projection with some of the principles of resonance.

Humming

Humming is one of the best exercises to help strengthen the voice. Bearing in mind preparation of alignment and posture, the following checkpoints should first be worked in slow motion:

– Gently lick the lips in case they are dry, and close them lightly.
– Drop the lower jaw inside them, remembering the tongue should stay flat and out of the way until needed.
– Let the tip of the tongue rest on the lower front teeth.
– From now on breath should be taken in through the mouth, being quicker and less noisy than through the nose; so open the mouth slightly and swing into a deep, wide breath.

– As you are ready for the return-swing out, lightly close the lips and
think of placing a full, easy sound on them.

If all is open and well, you will feel a vibration on the mask of the face, and
a considerable buzzing on the lips. They are likely to feel as a rabbit's nose
looks when it twitches, or when as a child you made a musical instrument by
intoning on a piece of tissue-paper folded over a comb.

If the buzzing is not felt immediately, allow time for breathing, sensation,
and placing to come together, which, for some people, can take a few weeks.
But there could be a degree of constriction somewhere, so try to ease it either
by some slight movement, or by almost feeling for the sound, in the head
and neck area. Another means of release is to lubricate the jaw, lips, and
cheeks by having a good chew on an imaginary piece of steak, or by being
lazily (but not literally) a cow chewing the cud. Then repeat the sound,
double-checking that the jaw is open inside the lips.

Here is another useful exercise to help bring the voice forward and
towards the mask of the face:

– Keeping the shoulders relaxed, raise the hands so that they are cupped
and almost within touching distance of the face.
– Take your breath as before, think the hum forward, and this time you
should feel the vibration falling into the palms of your hands. Or you
can get a similar sensation if you hold a thin piece of typing paper there.
– Repeat and, as you feel the buzz, gently extend your arms forward as if
you are pulling the sound out, as a conjuror pulls a rabbit from his hat.
As you let your hands finally drop to your sides, continue to think the
sound on and out, leaning it towards the far end of the room.

Combination of hum and open sound
Finally in this section of your voice routine, begin a blend of the hum with
the vocalized sigh.

– Check that the head and neck are free.
– Think of the sensation of the two sounds before you combine them.
– Take an easy breath and pass from a free, buzzing hum to the vocalized
sigh. Sustain each for 50 per cent of the total sound, one leaning
smoothly into the other.
– Nourish and support the sound with the breath from below; think of
continuing to listen to it until after it is actually over.

FIRST TRANSITION

This may be as far as you want to go for your first few sessions. But meanwhile you may be wondering how, with all this to consider for initial sounds, your routine relates to eventual use; you may also wonder whether the result will sound strange and artificial.

Remember that the routine is simply a means of gaining a first awareness and control of your voice. By starting simply, but getting the right feel of the breathing and initial sounds, you have some tangible points of departure. So by gaining an ease here, you can gradually apply and transpose it there. The next stage begins when you start to transpose the sensation into the connecting sounds that make up words, and then progress from sentences and on into paragraphs, into prose, poems, and plays or whatever.

But be patient, since in most other development of muscular use, such as sports or various forms of dancing, you are working at a new co-ordination adapted from everyday life. When it comes to the voice, however, you are working with an instrument that is an intrinsic part of your everyday life, and so the benefits from your routine may seem to fade occasionally and be hard to discern. You are rather like someone learning to touch-type by evening who meanwhile has to use the two-finger-and-look method by day. But if you establish the foundations carefully and without expecting immediate results, you can within a few months begin to gain a sense of new control and range in your speaking voice.

- So now try a long humming sound at the beginning of any word followed by an open vowel sound – for example, the name, 'Mmmmmmm-ary.'
- Check that you are sustaining the forward tone on these syllables and then try a line so familiar you don't have to think, 'Mary had a little lamb,' projecting it to the end of the room.
- Speak the name 'Mary' as you would conversationally a few times, maintaining projection and sense of the body leaning behind the voice.
- Speak the whole line conversationally.
- Speak the first and second lines on a breath:

Mary had a little lamb,
  Its fleece was white as snow;

When these fall into the room easily, add the third and fourth lines:

And everywhere that Mary went
  The lamb was sure to go.

– Play with it and, always keeping the voice free, juggle with the lines.

At least twice a week, do some reading aloud of good speaking material, with reference to the suggestions in later chapters. And as the months go by, continue to extend transition from exercise into experience.

4
Your Speaking Voice

We have now discussed an outline of the structure and function of the voice as a musical instrument able to produce tone. We have mentioned the importance of the positioning, or posture, of the whole body, with particular reference to the head, neck, and spine. (This is similar to the way a pianist, for example, considers the relationship of shoulders and arms to the rest of the body, so that all freedom and power may be released into the hands.) We have also reviewed the function of breathing, the making of sound in the larynx, and the development of resonance through effective use of the joint resonator of the throat, mouth, and nose.

So we are ready to investigate the gift of possessing not merely a tone-producing instrument, or voice, but a speaking voice which enables us to produce words. We will start with a reminder that words are composed of the sounds of speech, which fall into the categories of vowels and consonants.

Vowels

Vowels are continuous sounds, though some are longer than others. They are made with the voice and never just on the breath, as are some consonants; and are shaped by an open position of the resonator. So in contrast to consonants, which are made with a partial or sometimes complete closure within the mouth, vowels may be referred to as open sounds. Thus the flow is uninterrupted as the shape of the mouth moulds the tone, resulting in what in a sense can be regarded as the more musical part of our speech. It is sometimes noted by drama students, for example, that while music and feeling can be conveyed through vowel sounds, meaning can be conveyed through consonants.

One point is now likely to need clarification: within our context of speech we are dealing with sounds, not letters. Ordinary spelling would be mislead-

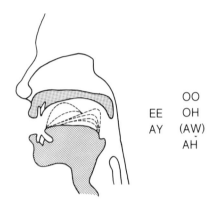

```
        OO
     EE OH
     AY (AW)
        AH
```

Figure 7 Position of the tongue
for the main long vowels

ing, for there are not enough letters in our alphabet to indicate all the sounds of our language. While there are only five vowel letters, a, e, i, o, u, they may, in combination with other letters, be pronounced in a variety of ways. For example, 'a' is pronounced one way in 'hat,' another in 'late,' and another in 'father.' In fact, in the speaking of various kinds of English, we may transpose our five vowel letters into over twenty different vowel sounds.

We will start with a look at the main long vowels, as they represent the furthermost positions of the tongue without its making any contact to help form a consonant. So they are an excellent means of practising the shaping and moulding of tone and, as you will find, of control of the tongue. If you think of all the languages in the world and of the multitude of their accents – what is termed cockney in English, for example having forty-three varieties – you will appreciate how very subtle the use and control of this muscle becomes.

THE MAIN LONG VOWELS

OO as in boot		and forward	tongue tip
OH as in boat	lips rounded	and wider	resting
(AW* as in bought)		and wider still	on
AH as in balm			lower
AY as in bay	lips relaxed		front
EE as in bee			teeth

As the aim is to keep the mouth as spherical as possible, you will see from the far right bracket that it is a golden rule to keep the tip of the tongue out of

* This position is used in parts of England, but is rare and can be omitted in North America.

the way and resting on the lower front teeth. Should the sphere become smaller than need be through raising the front or back of the tongue at the wrong time, or through the unnecessary closing of the jaw, much opportunity for resonance will be lost. Note that the jaw, which should be completely open and relaxed for AH, will want to close a little more for AY and EE, but the opening should never be so reduced that the teeth are touching. This is why a thumb's width is suggested for AY and EE; while the lips should be rounded to a whistle shape for OO, thumb shape for OH, and can be rounded as in SH for AW.

As you will find, these long vowel sounds form an essential part of daily practice, and are important because they help exercise the tongue, lip, and jaw muscles. But they are not necessarily among the sounds most commonly used. For example, the long 'a,' or AH, used in 'balm' is not as usual in North America as the short 'a' as in 'chance'; but it is representative of the flattest position of the tongue in the mouth and so carries out the purpose of the exercise. Come to know these sounds and their proper formation as you know your twice-times table; with good breathing they can form the basis of effective development of your speaking voice.

Included in these sounds is one used in parts of England, but having a variety of pronunciation elsewhere; this is AW as in 'bought,' in which the tongue is fairly flat at the back of the mouth. Here we have an example of using the advice 'When in Rome....' To request this sound, for example, in North America where it is not commonly used would be to impose a pronunciation that would be false to the current idiom. But knowledge of its formation is helpful to anyone who might need to adapt. Ideally, and in theory, it does not matter which version of a sound is used provided that it adheres to two main standards: that it is understood, and so is an aid and not a hindrance to communication; and that it is well produced. An ultra-English AW, for example, that is strangled in the back of a constricted throat, is just as much an impediment to clear speech as an ultra-North American version which can have a nasal resemblance to the quacking of a duck.

But speech, as we know, is not all a matter of pleasing sound. It must also make sense, and it is the stops, or breaks, provided by the consonants, which make for clarity, without which our speech would be one long, meaningless blur.

Consonants

Consonants are stops, or closures, partial or complete, between the lips, between the lips and teeth, or between any part of the tongue against the teeth, the teeth ridge, or the hard or soft palate. The consonant 's' is an example of a partial closure; with most people the tip of the tongue rises towards the back of the upper front teeth, though with some it curls down towards the lower front teeth. As a result, there is no complete closure or contact within the mouth. Rather it is through the light contact between tongue and teeth that the rush of breath sets up what is actually audible friction and accounts for the sibilant quality of the sound. Such friction is the aural equivalent of the tactile sense of the rush of your hand down a rope.

The tongue makes a similar partial contact, but more between the tongue tip and rims of the teeth, for 'th,' allowing the breath to escape with less friction. The result, when used as a substitute for 's,' is known as a lisp. In the 't' sound there is complete contact with the roof of the mouth. So this consonant acts as a form of complete stop to the column of air created by the outgoing breath.

There is another feature about consonants which clarifies their difference from vowel sounds. There are some pairs of consonants in which the two members are identically formed (b and p, or v and f) but have one voiced and one voiceless member. In other words, one member (b or v) uses vibration set up in the larynx, while the other (p or f) is whispered and projected on the breath alone. This division often comes as a surprise to people, and yet it is always interesting when something we have done as an unconscious, imitative habit all our lives is pointed out.

To illustrate, try the simple experiment of putting the back of your hand on the front of the larynx and making the sound, not saying the letter, 'f.' Do it again, holding it for a good, long puff. Provided you are making the sound and not saying the letter, you will not feel any vibration in the larynx. This time, make the sound, not the letter, for 'v,' and you should feel vibration under your hand. To be quite certain, make one long and three short 'v' sounds. Now alternate 'f' and 'v' sounds, and you should feel the vibrations turn on and off accordingly.

In the chart below you will find consonants listed under the main headings of place and manner of formation, such headings helping to clarify the difference between vowels and consonants. They are also a reminder to give full value to the voiced consonants, and to make good contact for those consonants formed by a complete closure. This is especially important in the case of the stops, or plosives, as opposed to the continuants.

It will be seen that the following pairs of voiced and voiceless consonants can also be classified as plosive sounds: b, p; d, t; g, k. They are formed by a three-part action known as closure, hold, and release. Working from the front to the back of the mouth, there is a closure between the lips (b, p),

Consonant Chart

Place of Closure	Partial closures			Complete closures		
		CONTINUANTS (Voiced)		PLOSIVES		
	FRICATIVE (Voiceless)	Oral	Nasal	Voiced	Voiceless	Jaw
Larynx	h					
Body of tongue and back of hard palate			ng	g	k	
						Open
Tongue tip and front of hard palate		l r,r (trill)	n	d	t	
Lips			m	b	p	
Lower lip and upper teeth	f	v				
						Partly Open
Tongue and upper teeth	th	th				
Tongue and upper or lower teeth	s	z				
Tongue and teeth, with lips	sh	zh				
						Closed
	Affricate					
Tongue and teeth with lips	ch	dzh				

between the tongue and the teeth ridge (d, t), and between the tongue and the soft palate (g, k). This contact is held briefly while the pressure of the breath and/or voice builds behind it; when this is greater than the muscle pressure holding the closure, the consonant is released, creating a particularly incisive sound. The clarity of these consonants depends on energy and co-ordination of muscle and breath; and speech is often considered lazy or inaudible when there is poor contact. If the closure is not held, or the breath does not build to create necessary pressure, the result is slurred. Conversely, if the action is too precise and careful, the result is pedantic and artificial; a useful guideline is in the saying that 'the height of art is to conceal art' or, in practical terms: 'IWBN' – in, without being noticeable.

Another sound which can require a careful balance between being over and underdone is the consonant 'r.' This is one of those interesting sounds which, according to different positions of the tongue, is pronounced in vari-

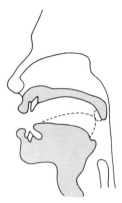

Figure 8 French uvular rolled 'r'

ous ways in different languages and dialects, and within their accents, or variants. For example, 'r' in French is a rolled sound produced by the undulation of the tongue and soft palate, or uvula.

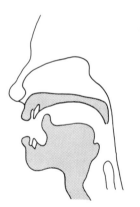

Figure 9 British fricative 'r'

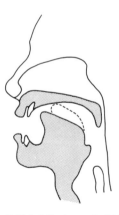

British trilled or rolled 'r'

The 'r' in British English is of two kinds. One is called fricative, in which the tip of the tongue is raised towards the teeth ridge. The other is known by the woodpecker term of a one-tap trill, in which the tip briefly taps the ridge, and is used most in words where it comes between two vowel sounds, such as ve*r*y or me*rr*y.

In some areas of Scotland the 'r' tends to be trilled, or even rolled, all the time, and in others it is left out and substituted by a glottal shock, which has nothing to do with the tongue position. The glottal shock is an actual speech sound in the German language, where it may be used before vowel sounds, and is composed of a stop of breath within the glottis, or space between the vocal cords. There will be more about this sound in the voice routine at the end of this chapter.

In North America the 'r' is a variant of the fricative 'r,' and is sometimes made with the tongue raised far back in the mouth, strangling the tone and giving an impression of heaviness to the speech. Such a gripping of sound by the tongue can, however, be used to good account when applied to a style of delivery used in some commercials in radio or television advertising.

Occasionally, speakers with some types of speech on either side of the Atlantic have comparatively little 'r' in their pronunciation. The tongue tends to waver around in the middle of the mouth while compensation is attempted by substituting another sound, often the labial, or lip-sound, 'w.' If wished, this can be corrected in time and with practice by creating an awareness and control of the tongue through strengthening exercises; and with many people the best position for the tongue can finally be found by working from the position most near. This is the consonant 'n,' from which the 'r' can be reached by allowing the tip of the tongue to drop back and down by less than half a centimetre. However, it is one thing to do this in concentrated isolation, but more difficult to incorporate it in the flow of connected speech.

A further classification of consonants comes under the heading of continuants, as opposed to the plosive sounds. These too may be voiced as in '*th*is,' or voiceless as in '*th*ink.' Being continuant they are naturally longer than the stopped sounds, and the voiced continuants in particular are useful in aiding the resonance of the vowel sounds, and so helping to carry the tone.

Articulation

Whereas the quality of resonance in speech is primarily concerned with vowel sounds, articulation is primarily concerned with consonants. This adaptation of the resonating cavity of the mouth as a shaper of vowels and an articulator of consonants is a sophisticated process which took man millions of years to evolve. It still takes individual man approximately the first five years of his life to synchronize the sound and structure of language to begin to achieve effective, two-way communication. Such a development is dependent on an intricate co-ordination of mind and muscle, which is physically controlled by the sense of rhythm. And, as voice is the sound, so speech reflects the rhythm, of the personality.

But speech, like other forms of human behaviour, can change within the attitudes and conditions of society. For example, in the elocutionary days of the turn of the century, there was a tendency to think of over-clear articulation as the aim of effective speech. The emphasis was on delivery, rather than on content, and it was more important to be impressed by the style of the speaker than to receive a clear impression of his message. The result could be pedantic and plummy, and often arose out of the 'how-now-brown-cow' and the 'pear-shaped-tones' schools of speech.

Meanwhile three major factors have helped change this fashion: the development of effective training in speech, which was largely pioneered by professional theatre schools in England, and in the United States by university departments of speech; the democratization and levelling of society; and recent developments in technology which facilitate speech communication. All of which, in turn, are beginning to lead to a more balanced use of speaking and writing in schools.

Electronic amplification and broadcast of the voice have led to a reduction in the need for over-emphasis in articulation. Clarity of speech must still, however, be used with a sense of proportion. Too little, and the result is untidy and prevents ease of communication; too much and the tendency, for opposite reasons, is for the listener to listen out. Again a reminder that the standard best applied is IWBN – in, without being noticeable.

The amalgam of sounds uttered by the speaking voice now needs to be drawn together, for once early practice is established they should not be considered as separate entities. So it is time to look at a cohering element which enables an effective speaker to give a special attribute to whoever good words he may speak. It seems that few people, with perhaps the exception of actors, some preachers, teachers, and poets, think of words in terms of their total significance of sound, or music, as well as of their sense.

The musical significance of sound

This is a useful term to remember in giving an inherent value and balance to the everyday sounding of vowels and consonants; for when blended within an effective selection of words, they become a vital medium in the orchestration of speech. A sense of the musical significance is helpful to all users of words, who are, after all, still 'dealers in magic and spells,' and this special factor is also used by many writers who often double-check the full complement of sound and meaning by reading their work aloud. It is of interest, perhaps, that so valued is this particular significance of words that the editor-in-chief of a large publishing firm once claimed he could tell how musical writers are by reading one paragraph of their work.

But all users of the musicality and balance of sound can benefit from a particular spin-off, which could be termed a relish for words. This appears not for its own sake, but to help share the speaker's particular taste for the image they convey. Words spoken without relish are, 'weary, stale, flat and unprofitable' to listen to. Imagine the difference between eating an egg without salt and pepper and then with them; or imagine a hamburger without trimmings and then with them. So it is with words, that they must be sounded as if visualizing the image of their meaning if the full significance of a passage is to be conveyed.

Consider, for example, the word 'grave,' which either as noun or adjective has a decidedly solemn meaning. It also has a rich couple of sounds at the beginning, 'g' and 'r' both being voiced, with that first plosive being released through the following continuant. Most of us give full value to these. Then comes the simple vowel AY with which we are already familiar. But now listen to that 'v' at the end; on the chart it is a voiced continuant. Is that how you make it? If it were, however, to become the voiceless equivalent, or 'f,' the result would make the word sound as 'grafe.' This would lack the natural colour implied by the shading of this particular word, for ideally meaning and music work together, one continually complementing the other.

Further illustration of this point involves a rule which may be a useful reminder to everyday users as well as to newcomers to the language: when the plural 's' is added to the end of a word, it usually takes the voiced or voiceless colouring of the previous sound. It should be stressed again that this means sound, not letter, which in our non-phonetic spelling can often be mute. Thus when 'grave' is used as a noun, and 'v' is the last sound rather than the letter 'e,' when the plural is added it is pronounced 'z' rather than 's.'

If we look at the word 'king,' the same rule applies. It ends with the voiced nasal consonant 'ng,' so when made plural the 's' is pronounced 'z.' To consider the value of this point in the full context of sound and meaning, try such a plural in a famous line such as Shakespeare's 'This sceptr'd isle, this throne of kings.' The result would hardly give the impression of much of a throne if the end of the word 'kings' was lost in an 's.' But when influenced by that previous voiced consonant, then it has a chance of conveying full value to sound and meaning.

It cannot be too clearly stressed, however, that if words were merely to be mouthed for the sake only of their sound, the result would draw more attention to their manner than to their matter, and would hinder rather than help communication. But an understanding of the various types of sound, and so of their contribution to a context, can be as helpful to the speaker as a knowledge of various instruments and their range to a musician.

The result can be best used when imagination joins forces with technique. Savour that word 'grave' again. You know technically now about the value of the 'v' at the end, and that if practised well it should adhere to our standard of IWBN, so that it is there in right proportion, as one hundred pence to a pound or cents to a dollar. Then, by using the imagination, think of a carrying image such as a deserted graveyard on a dull winter's day and add your own details as to weather, colouring, and city or country background. Try the word a few times. Gradually you will find that with total concentration and immersion it quietly speaks true, and can convey a total image from speaker to listener. Use of the speaking voice is not an end in itself, but is simply a channel or a medium through which the total significance of a passage can be conveyed.

To be effective, good words must be so nourished if they are to be well spoken. We now turn to a look at one further element in the use of the speaking voice which will help ensure the vital factor of its audibility.

Projection

Projection is literally the throwing out of sound and meaning so that the full impact of words can be not only heard but also understood by all sorts of listeners under all types of conditions.

This is a tall order; but it is also an essential link in the development of an effective speaking voice. Unfortunately, with contemporary dependence on amplification by microphone, some speakers feel little need to consider what happens to their listeners if ever this medium is lacking or goes wrong. But just as it is a wise move for every driver to be able to control a car with a gearshift, and not always depend on automatic, every speaker should be able to control his own projection. This is not a matter of shouting, which would be a strain to the speaker and harsh to the listener, but of effective enlargement of sound and of concentrated intent of meaning. Technically it is dependent on all we have so far discussed, and more, and is unlikely to be sustained for long without certain prerequisites. These include careful attention to relaxation, posture, and breathing; which in turn can support a balanced resonance and clear articulation. And, needless to say, no one should ever know you have been practising. Gradually initial effort will lessen, a new conscious control will become automatic, and good habit will become established.

Ideally, when projection is effective, the speaker's voice, as that of a singer, appears to be used without effort so that it carries with ease to the proverbial back row. Sound and meaning will then seem to take place, not within the body of the speaker, but virtually within the body of listeners, whether composed of a small group, or of a large audience or congregation, so that it seems to carry personally to every individual. In a way the process is similar to the enlargement of a small print in photography. This implies that not only must the technical wherewithal be good, but focus must first be clear and sharp. So it is with the meaning of a passage. Unless the speaker has the intent clearly in mind and heart, the outline of meaning will be fuzzy when enlarged. There is a saying which is valuable here: 'Be sure mind is in gear before setting speech in motion.'

Voice routine

Begin with a time of preparation, include relaxation and a check of previous work on movement and posture.

BREATHING
In the initial breathing exercises your aim was to increase flexibility and rib-swing. Now it is time to adapt this everyday rhythm to that required for speech, and so begin to work on a quick, silent intake and a slow, steady output.

– Breathe in through an open, relaxed mouth on a silent count of 1, and breathe out counting aloud 1-2-3-4-5-6. Continue to release any residue of breath-pressure on a whispered sigh.
– Checkpoints: the ingoing breath should be inaudible. If there is a gasp, it can be caused by a slight tension constricting the tongue, which originates just above the larynx, so narrowing what should be an open throat. The ingoing breath, instead of rushing freely, scrapes a bit. The gasp you hear is audible friction, similar in sound to the sensation of running your hand down a rope.
– Let the counts on the outgoing breath be as free and open as the previous sensation of your vocalized sigh, and use them at the rate of approximately one per second. Sustain the sound of each so that it falls continuously into the next.
– Over a period of two to three months increase the outgoing counts to 9, 12, 16, 20, 25, 30.

- Maintain the idea of the weight of the body behind the voice.
- Think of your breath as supporting the sound throughout the room; as resonance develops, you can even imagine it making a gentle bulge in walls and ceiling.
- Once you are up to about twenty counts with ease, combine breathing and voicing with other forms of movement: walking on the spot, walking and moving, and then changing direction with a new breath.

By combining movement with voice you can gradually check that all remains flexible and the sound free; though this can take a while to achieve. Initially, for example, the voice may become quiet and almost disappear when you are thinking about and doing other things. But as it begins to work easily under practice conditions, you will hopefully never have to think about it during actual delivery.

PRACTICE OF VOWEL SOUNDS
If you check back to the section on vowels earlier in this chapter, you will find a working outline of the main long vowel sounds, OO, OH, (AW,) AH, AY, EE.

- You are already familiar with the most open of them, AH, from your voiced sigh. Being sure the jaw is open, go from there to OO. Try the movement from one to the other in slow motion. Take a good breath to sustain the sound, so that as the OO looks like a whistle, you feel you could almost bore a hole in the wall opposite you. Maintain support through that sense of the leaning of body and breath, rather than through any sense of muscular constriction or push.
- Work on the OO on its own, and when it feels easy and can be sustained on a long breath, progress to the OH; and take a couple of weeks to concentrate on these initial sounds.
- As you come to AY and EE, try to avoid any sense of the once popular 'smile-and-say-cheese' approach to speech, in which the jaw was closed and the sound released through a tight grin. You will gain better resonance if you aim for a relaxed, open jaw, with the mouth sufficiently wide open to allow the top joint of the thumb to be popped in and out vertically. This will come through keeping the cavity of the mouth open, rather than through an unnecessary tense-and-widen around the lips, which can, in turn, affect the muscles of the neck and the voice.
- Continue to practise shaping the vowels in conjunction with good breathing. Sustain them singly and in pairs and more, for the 9, 12, or whatever counts you can achieve without effort.

- To maintain forward placing of the voice it is helpful to use a hum as a springboard before any of these sounds; but always check for that sensation of a good buzz on the lips before continuing to the vowel.
- You can relate production of the main vowels to everyday use by adding to and practising your own list of words that contain them. Then put these into sentences, or create your own rhymes or patter exercises, to add to those later in the text.
- Another way is to think of a selected vowel sound for a few minutes each day. By listening to and observing how other people use the EE sound, for example, and noticing whether they tighten or open the jaw, you can become more aware of your own use of the sound in everyday situations.

GLOTTAL SHOCKS

The glottis, as you will remember from the earlier description, is the space between the vocal cords. When all works well, we automatically close it at the beginning of a voiced sound in timing with the onset of breath. But sometimes we close the glottis and then apply the breath. So additional pressure has to be used for the breath to push, rather than pass easily between, the inner edges of the vocal cords. The action sets up a series of small jerks, or shocks, and can be due to lack of co-ordination caused by tension at one level or fatigue at another. If the tendency becomes habitual, it can give an impression of toughness, or set in to become part of the growl known as a gravel voice.

While the glottal shock occurs as a legitimate speech sound in some languages, it rarely appears in English except as a stop, or form of consonant, in some regional accents. There is famed use of it preceding the vowel in the German 'Achtung!', and the rhythm of some oriental languages is tuned to this different timing of sound and breath. But you can hear a glottal shock substituted for a mid-plosive consonant such as 't,' for example, in some areas of Scotland and in some forms of cockney in words such as 'butter' and 'little.'

- Should you become aware of some hardness of attack at the beginning of your work on individual vowel sounds, or on whole words beginning with a vowel, it can be eased through temporary use of an opposite co-ordination, and then by re-timing it anew. For example:
- Start by letting out a lot of breath, or an H as for a sigh, before each vowel sound:

large sigh	H-OO H-OH (H-AW) H-AH H-AY H-EE
medium sigh	h-OO h-OH (h-AW) h-AH h-AY h-EE
inaudible sigh	(h)OO (h)OH ((h)AW) (h)AH (h)AY (h)EE

Everyone can afford to check this co-ordination every few weeks. We are all subject to occasional pressures, and it is easy to let a small amount of tension develop into a tightness of voice, which can affect the way we relate to people. Particularly for those whose jobs depend on the way they speak in public, awareness of the glottal shock can be a way of detecting unrecognized tension which can constrain the full potential of the voice.

PRACTICE OF CONSONANTS

You have already added one consonant, M, to the main vowel sounds, and you can now add combinations of the whole range of consonants. But it is helpful to realize that while this section of your routine will continue to require inner concentration and a good sense of rhythm, it should not be taken at too serious a plod. At a superficial level, for example, the sounding of DAHs and DOOs, while fun to practise in a group, can make for an initial sense of awkwardness if working on your own. But keep in mind the aim of polishing co-ordination, ready for transition into everyday use, and such exercises become similar to scales for a singer, warm-ups for an athlete, or barre work for a ballet dancer. Aim for precision without tension, but with flexibility and forward placing.

Work through the consonants, grouping them if you wish from the list in this chapter, but starting with the liquid sound, L, as it makes for good exercise of the tongue.

– Check that the mouth is open, so it is the tongue that works rather than the jaw that flops up and down:
  LOO LOH (LAW) LAH LAY LEE
– Then use the plosives for good contact, working from the front to the back of the mouth, and in pairs according to whether they are voiced or voiceless: B,P; D,T; G,K.
– As you use them in words and exercises, you are likely to find the voiceless plosives can be taken more quickly and lightly than the voiced, and an exploration of these sounds can help give you a greater awareness of their value in the orchestration of connected speech.
  voiced   BOO BOH (BAW) BAH BAY BEE
  voiceless   POO POH (PAW) PAH PAY PEE
– Then try the continuants including V and F and Z and S:
  voiced   VOO VOH (VAW) VAH VAY VEE
  voiceless   FOO FOH (FAW) FAH FAY FEE
– As all continues rhythmically, aim for flexibility by using different speeds. Then progress to random choice of any consonant at the beginning and the end of the main vowel:

DOOB DOHB (DAWB) DAHB DAYB DEEB
- As rhythm stays in control and courage develops, add more:
  ZDOOBV ZDOHBV (ZDAWBV) ZDAHBV ZDAYBV ZDEEBV
- Keep going, hang on to your hat, and if you achieve more than three or four at either end, treat yourself for shock.
- Vowels and consonants can also be practised in different combinations for the percussive effects of the plosives, by using these, for example, in triplicate before each vowel:
  GGG-GOO GGG-GOH (GGG-GAW) GGG-GAH GGG-GAY GGG-GEE
- Should any jerkiness or slurring occur in such exercises, return to where all was under control and then pick up the speed again.

If you feel you are not giving full value to some sounds, try working at them in isolation. For example, some people lack grip of the consonant 'r'; in which case check that lip movement is not substituted for tongue movement, as described earlier in this chapter. Then try it within a combination of nonsense sounds, as above, and it will gradually be ready for everyday use.

ARTICULATION EXERCISES
Now your routine begins to warm towards putting all such preparation into sounds of some continuity and significance.

- Try reading the following light verse aloud three or four times, and after a few days see if you can do three or four lines on a breath, while still making the meaning sound easy.
- Give the lines the bubble and zest of the spirit in which they were written, exploring the mock-earnestness of such a dire situation:

To sit in solemn silence in a dull, dark dock;
In a pestilential prison with a life-long lock,
Awaiting the sensation of a short, sharp shock,
From a cheap and chippy chopper on a big black block.

From *The Mikado*, Gilbert and Sullivan

If you are not sure whether the word-endings are clear, whisper the lines. Not as a forced, loud, vocalized sort of whisper, but lightly and gently. You will soon hear whether the consonants are there, and not overdone, yet in proportion to need.

After whispering, put the voice back lightly, and your ear will be more perceptive about the quality of your own, and possibly of other people's, articulation.

DEVELOPMENT OF PROJECTION
As you feel confidence developing in breathing, ease of posture, and range of voice, begin to allot a section of your routine to projection. For example:

- From the carrying sound M, open on to a lip-rounded OO or OH, and aim the dual sound half way across the room.
- Then think it to the back of the room, so that your voice seems to take place as much out there as in you.
- If possible, find a larger space occasionally, such as an empty meeting-room or small auditorium, and do the same; never forcing the sound, but mentally and physically directing it.
- You will become somewhat like a tennis player who maintains control and direction of the ball even when playing from way behind the back line.

As the pinpointing of meaning and feeling travels easily on the carrying wave of your voice, try to gain some practice in a medium-to-large hall or auditorium, preferably with a partner or group of other people. As you stand on a platform or stage, check any impulse to take a breath and belt the words to the back row with little sense of subtlety. Likewise, avoid any tendency to tilt the head back and, even after some months of preparation, note any muscular constriction sometimes linked with a sense of effort when trying something new.

- Before you begin, take an easy breath or two.
- Remember the points about posture, and allow a moment of concentration while you gather your resources.

Then, instead of thinking straight to the back, which may look a wind-tunnel of distance away, bear in mind that as sound waves travel, they can ricochet like a bullet. This form of reverberation replenishes their force. So, while you need not actually look down, think of the sound as making contact with a hard surface, such as the floor, about halfway to the back. Experiment with this sense of bouncing the sound waves off a helpful surface, say, one-third and two-thirds, along on their journey, and you can gain some sense of contact on the way, rather than having to encompass the whole space with one total throw of your voice.

Always think in terms of talking naturally to someone, and avoid any temptation to shout. But if your enlargement of sound is to be effective, remember that it will take infinitesimally longer to reach someone at a distance. Make that nth degree of allowance in your pace, support all of it by good breathing, and you will establish a valuable first response to the needs of your listeners.

Then develop the use of projection while reading aloud.

5

The Flow of Your Connected Speech

We have considered the structure and function of the speaking voice, and the human ability to turn isolated sounds into words, and it is time to investigate the different ways through which we control our uniquely human instrument during the flow of connected speech.

Such control includes three vital factors: an innate sense of co-ordination, an intricate series of movements synchronized by rhythm, and a fine tuning of the whole by a use of the ear so automatic it is barely conscious. An idea of the marvel of the process which leads to this sounding of our being can be gained from a look at its development.

Development and co-ordination

The baby is born with a voice and with it soon learns to attract attention, for in addition to facial expression and first movements, it is a certain means of communication. Sounds of need, gurgles of appreciation, and cries of anger and frustration are associated with results. As the brain develops, there is a wish to express on a clearer level, and so comes the ability to arrange and control a fascinating process of muscular movement; he kicks, grasps, and holds with growing strength. Soon gurgles turn into syllables, and syllables are jumbled into the, to adults, non-recognizable words of baby-language, often understood by small children. He transmits the primitive sound of his voice into speech through unconsciously learning to imitate the family use of muscles, including those of the lips, jaw, and tongue. As he begins to stand, and to toddle, his speech toddles too; trying the repetition of syllables at a run and falling over them, resulting in apparently meaningless but enjoyable experiments. He takes delight in repetition and in the sheer sound of words, which can sadly be lost in later years. As he continues to explore the use of arms, legs, fingers, and toes, he is also beginning to discover the co-ordination of those muscles concerned with speech.

As the brain becomes more active, the newly acquired habit of speech can be put to fascinating use and, because it is much dependent on the process of hearing as well as to some extent on seeing, the general style and melody remains that of the family. Then come the particular tunes of rhymes and jingles which are continually requested, and here lies a double and instinctive wisdom. Speech, as we know, is muscular movement, and all movement, whether the swing of an athlete or the intricate co-ordination of a pianist, is controlled by rhythm. Thus rhythm helps pattern the memory and helps to lay the foundation of a growing knowledge of intelligible sounds. It also helps provide a vocabulary, which will one day become the fundamental tool for sharing all the thoughts and feelings that a human being can convey.

So from purposeful nonsense and the occasional long-winded word which the four-year-old tries out with such pride, evolve discoveries of what a child is thinking and feeling, and companionship can be established. This is followed by an age of perpetual inquiry, and 'what?' 'why?' and 'where?' spice the conversation. Speech becomes a means of finding acceptance by and of others; and the person inside the child becomes evident.

Physically, once first teeth appear, the tongue learns to articulate, joining syllables into words and remembering, unconsciously now, how to move it towards or away from the teeth, or from the hard or soft palates. The second teeth grow, and by the age of seven or eight the acquired habit of speech will, like handwriting, begin to reflect the evolving personality.

Interests widen, hobbies appear, and the ability to read both silently and aloud develops. The entire process of muscular co-ordination has a few years in which to evolve a sure sense of control and strength until the final period of physical growth. Then with adolescence comes a time of physical change, during which it is important that neither the singing nor the speaking voice of either boys or girls is strained. Parallel with a first awareness of society as a whole, a total pattern of interest and attitudes develops. A major adjustment to work takes place while the core of the personality, and of vocal habits, is formed.

Gradually this co-ordination of messages through the central nervous system and the continual contraction and relaxation of muscle fibre is best co-ordinated within the flow of rhythm. For, as we make and use machines to operate rhythmically – for even changing gears on a car needs rhythm – so we control our movements, and so our speech. You will find, for example, that even the first breathing exercises should be rhythmic, and then this initial swing can be adapted to the more complicated rhythms of continuous speech.

To appreciate the importance of this point, consider what it would be like to listen to speech that is non-rhythmic and jerky. Not only would the result hamper the flow, but it could also make for a feeling of unease in the listener and be a detriment to clear communication. Conversely, a delivery in which the rhythm is too regular can result in monotony; but as with our discussion of meaning and sound, when meaning and rhythm go hand-in-hand, each quality complements the other.

Ear training

It is helpful to consider the ear as the eye of the voice, for just as an artist trains his eye to become vibrantly aware of form, line, and colour, so you will find that the speaker needs to become equally aware of all rises, falls, and nuances of the voice.

But because the process is so automatic and immediate, it is not often realized that the ear must perceive before a sound can be truly reproduced. Sometimes bringing to mind the tune or accent we wish to use is difficult, and we consciously have to try to perceive the sound within our inner ear before we can sing or speak our intentions to others. This ability is called the mental perception of sound, and it should be as carefully nurtured in developing the speaking voice as it is in training the singing voice. When there is need for some repetition of practice, such concentration helps avoid a hit-or-miss quality. So hearing ahead and using this watchdog of control helps the result to sound as intended.

For example, even when using the simple 'AH' sound during practice of the vowel sounds, it is soon helpful to aim not only for a certain pitch, but also for the degree of volume you require. Then you have your own yard-stick by which to begin to measure your results, and gradually you can try to pre-set the instrument so that the voice will reflect all requirements. But again it is essential to be sure of what and how we wish to speak before we begin to communicate; for as in comments on projection, a fuzzy sound perceived is likely to be a fuzzy sound reproduced, so again be sure 'mind is in gear ....'

In some cases it may also be necessary to ensure that the original perception of hearing is good, and any doubt as to hearing ability should be checked early in the development of the speaking voice. Some people find it hard to tell the difference between a high and a low note easily, and may think that they are tone-deaf; and if a doctor confirms a hearing loss, all care should be taken in diagnosis and treatment. But this is a comparatively rare defect, often sadly traceable to advice to stop singing because the work of a choir is being held back. Such lack of encouragement can lead to inability to concentrate and to lack of effort in trying to distinguish between one sound or note from another; but if there is a wish to develop an ear which may have been latent, the ability can be restored with time and effort. First there is need to concentrate on perceiving extremes, such as high and low notes on a piano; then to begin to reproduce them; then to try and perceive intervals, and to reproduce them, until it is possible to sing or hum a scale. Finally, from the clearly defined notes of music, the ear can become more attuned to the perception and the reproduction of the subtleties of speech.

It will be found, however, that some ear training should become part of any voice routine. It will involve continual use of this inward ear, by hearing before making sounds; of practice of scales and some singing; of reading aloud; and of trial and experiment with words, lines, and speeches. And while all such activity is an aid to control, it is as well to remember that the fascinating process of hoping your voice will sound as you intend is a never-ending quest. Rather than a facility that comes alive and settles into place for life, it needs perpetual awareness and practice, and constant use of that particular muscle of concentration which enlivens the context or the situation of a passage. Everyone can experience that will-o'-the-wisp elusiveness when the inner ear knows exactly how words should sound only to find the result is not as wished. So it is important for both listeners and speakers to work to surmount any barriers of so-called wooden voices and tin ears – which can go with expressionless faces. Communication is a continuing challenge, and a growing technique which includes breathing and ear training will gradually provide some of the means through which full expression may be shared.

Finding the middle note

One of the factors which helps give a sense of control to the flow and range of your connected speech can be discovered through ear training. This involves finding the middle note of your speaking voice, which is mainly dependent on the length and thickness of your particular vocal cords. The note is altered partly by the ear and partly by the varying degree of pull, or tension, of the cords, and is also influenced by the power of the breath which sets them vibrating.

It is possible to establish your natural range by singing down a comfortable scale to the last low note that is easy to reach without growl or effort. About four notes above that low note is your middle speaking note; this is usually almost a third lower in men than in women, or say middle C as compared to E or E flat above. Since the proportion of our compass is, in theory, the same, what can be accomplished four notes down can also be accomplished four notes up. The natural range of the speaking voice is approximately eight notes, or an octave, and of the average singing voice approximately sixteen notes, or two octaves.

Because it is comparatively easy for the untrained speaker to compress a high note, and through lack of experience to assume that the result is the starting-point from which to come down, it is always safer to establish that middle note, or mean degree of tension, first.

It is important that the speaking voice is never strained in relation to this natural compass, and to remember that the result is largely a matter of comparison. No one voice can be called high unless it is thought higher than the average, or low unless for the opposite reason. It can be particularly unfortunate if teenagers are told by untrained opinion that they have a high voice, and are merely told to lower the pitch. The voice may seem high for reasons connected with poor use, such as constriction of the resonator and/or poor breathing, which can lead to a particularly thin and apparently high sound. But deliberately to lower what is already a partially strained voice will overstrain it even further, and could lead to serious and lasting trouble; and since the voice is a reflection of both physique and personality, effective development should be responsive to both.

Intonation

Another factor present in the flow of all speaking voices, and a major channel to affect the reaction of listeners, is intonation. This means the total tune or spoken melody of connected speech, and brings together the major elements of how things are said. As one of the best ways to develop your ear is to balance awareness by listening to the tune of others, you will find that every individual has a slightly different melody. (To a degree members of the same tribe will sound similar for, in addition to the process of speech being imitative, there is also the matter of similar bone structure.) People who come from the same region and use an accent, or variant, of their language, also sound similar. But when the melody is widely different from your own, you are usually hearing a change not only of accent, but of the whole spoken idiom of the language of another country. Consider the difference in melody between French and German, or Dutch and Italian; or the difference in stress between German, which usually has a firm, dogmatic sound, and Russian which can be particularly fluid and musical. Then bring to your mind's ear some of the many varieties of your own language, including perhaps the long twist of vowels in part of the southern United States, or the upward lilt in Wales, or the clipped finality of some British English compared to the less formal tune of most North American English.

Within this total pattern of melody it is helpful to look at the parts. These include inflection, or the rise and fall of the voice, which colours words in passing from one pitch to another. This is the quality which, particularly on the final word, helps give clarity to such intent as the questioning, encouraging, or even discouraging of others; and upon which we clamp down when there is need to be non-committal. Pitch is also greatly reflective of mood and feeling, for within our individual range we all tend, for example, to use a high pitch, and a fast pace, when excited and a low pitch and slow pace when sad.

An interesting point about pace, or the rate at which we speak, is that any need to quicken should not be confused with gabbling, or headlong rush without pause. For a pause can have special value, and may be defined as a cessation of voice but never of thought or feeling, which is why it is sometimes considered more eloquent than words. Then there is volume, or loudness or softness of the voice; and finally it is interesting to remember that these parts may be grouped together under the heading of modulation, which is a musical term meaning to change from one key to another.

Being aware of such factors is helpful when we wish to check modulation for control and variety. If you feel that your voice is monotonous, and every speaker can fall into this vocal rut occasionally, it is useful to listen to the way in which others make a fresh point by starting on a different pitch; or to become aware that the voice should maintain volume at the end of a phrase, as otherwise there is recurring inaudibility. Needless to say, attempts to develop range and interest could become artificial if merely used for the sake of going up here and down there. Ideally the aim should be a flexible voice which will reflect the needs of a situation.

It is also useful to remember that all factors which help modify the voice are interrelated. For example, without enough breath the pitch would tend to drop; through lack of power there could be a repeated falling inflection; pace could be dragged because of the effort required to take in further breath; tone become thin and pinched for lack of support, and articulation seem lazy and without enough power for the plosive consonants. There would be little change of volume because most of it would be soft, and the whole mechanism would be in as sorry a state as an organ without air in the bellows, for good breathing lies at the heart of an effective voice. So also does general health, and the above symptoms could, if extreme, be caused by severe depression or some form of physical or mental breakdown.

But on a more positive note, the melodic pattern of English tends to fall within three major tunes: upward, used at commas and indicating continuity, or used at some question marks and indicating query; downward, indicating finality at full stops and used to a more marked degree at the end of paragraphs; and compound, being an up-down or a down-up blend of the first and second tunes which reflects doubt, irony, and a further element, hopefully rarely used or heard, of sarcasm.

Stress, meaning and form

Whereas in some languages, such as Chinese, meaning can be imparted by subtle variations in pitch, meaning in all the variations of the English language is imparted by intonation and also by stress, or emphasis, according to the importance of a word in the total context. Were each word to be given equal stress, the result would be as rocky as a road under construction, and just as difficult for the listener to pass along; conversely, lack of stress would be the equivalent of a lack of any path of meaning.

There are, however, about forty small words forming conjunctions which are usually less important than the verbs and nouns they join. For example, try pronouncing separately, 'was,' 'to,' and 'the.' Now put them in the flow of a sentence, stressing the final noun, 'he was going to the party.' Try it again and you may notice that the vowel in 'was' becomes shortened and is pronounced in a neutral position, as used in the first syllable of the word 'about.' You are likely to find the same thing happening with the vowel in the word 'to,' which is also shortened as the word becomes less strong and so is pronounced in what is known as its 'weak' form. The process is usually repeated in the next word, 'the.'

The result may seem small in theory but it is important in practice, and can be specially important to newcomers to the language. But even though we probably conform to this habit quite easily in everyday speech we should realize it exists so that we may also use it with proportion when, for example, projecting or reading aloud. Use of a strong instead of the weak and more natural form can sound artificial and can occur under the mistaken impression of gaining clarity of articulation. The result can also change meaning, for use of the strong form in 'was' is likely to gain stress, and if this happens in 'he *was* going to the party' it gives an implication that there was doubt about his going.

But the mature use of any form of stress is not merely a matter of weight on a word or of the old gag about 'the em*phas*is being on the right syl*lab*le.'

Rather the aim is again IWBN, and stress is most effective when used with other factors that make speech not only informative but also interesting to listen to.

Speech accents

Accents are a fascinating topic, and with the world shrinking to the size of a village in terms of accessibility and time involved in travel, it is as well to remember that everyone, being from somewhere, has an accent to the ears of one from somewhere else.

Accents come in three major categories, of which one is regional, or that version of a language spoken within a geographic boundary. For example, it used to be said that to speak one of the many varieties of genuine cockney it was necessary to have been born within the sound of Bow Bells, or within a mile of the church in the London parish of St Mary-le-Bow. An accent may also be national, as spoken within the boundaries of another country using the same language, but in turn possessing its own variants. Hence the varieties of Scottish English, Welsh English, or Australian or South African English. Each variant can also have its own mini-language, or dialect, which may be unintelligible to other users, such as the rhyming slang of cockney, or whole phrases and twists of voice of Geordie, spoken in Newcastle-on-Tyne in the north of England.

The third category of accents may be termed linguistic, or that version of a language coloured by the first language of the speaker. For example, some mid-European languages, such as Czech, do not have the sound 'ng,' and in an attempt to interpret our spelling phonetically, the result is often a carefully made 'nk.' So 'ring' tends to become 'rink' and 'singing' becomes 'singkingk.' Similarly, people from Germany do not use the sound 'w' and confuse it with their nearest version which is 'v,' so that 'welcome' tends to become 'velcome.' Such examples illustrate an interesting point about one of the factors of human fallibility for, unless specially perceptive, we find it hard to hear, and thus to reproduce, those sounds that we do not ourselves make.

So just as we would find it hard to distinguish many sounds of Oriental languages, many people from the Orient are mystified by our consonant 'r' and resort to, to them, the nearest identifiable sound of 'l'; and so the phrase 'very dry' becomes 'velly dly.' Closer to home, there tends to be an understandable lack of connection between some sounds of British English and North American English. Non-hearing of the unaccustomed plays a part in a misconception which again concerns the 'r,' for since North Americans don't use a British version, or that one-tap trill between vowels, they assume the result is their nearest equivalent, or the plosive consonant 'd.' Hence their comment about people being 'veddy British.' Conversely the British, often realizing there is something a little different about the North American 'r,' which unlike theirs is always fricative and pronounced wherever written, tend to change the vowel sound and to compensate by talking of people as being 'vury Amurican.'

Matters of accent, however, are far more than details of pronunciation. Fundamentally they are a reflection of the personality and the culture of a nation or a region, as reflected in the rhythms and stress, and other factors involved in the flow of their connected speech. And just as some people have that happy gift for playing music by ear, others have a special co-ordination, blessed by a naturally perceptive ear to the totality of other sounds and accents, which make them born linguists. Naturally adaptive, they can also take delight in becoming so much a part of another culture and expression, that it is interesting to see how their personalities change and become chameleon to the whole range of voice, attitude, and gesture until, instead of sounding stilted and foreign, they often achieve the impression of being native born.

Vocal signals and their development

Vocal signals indicate the shifts of feeling and of thought that are continually reflected in the sound of the voice. They are as ancient as the caveman, and still form an underlying system within the flow of our connected speech that is a basic ingredient of our communicating lives. So automatic are they that we now use them unconsciously, though perhaps with some awareness when voicing, rather than talking, to animals and babies.

So intrinsic are they to what may be termed our oral/aural vocabulary – for we usually only make and hear sounds within our normal listening range – that through them we also perceive the subtle and general changes of mood in others. For example, the better you know people, the more their voices, and not just their speech, talk to you; and if used to phoning them more than a few times a week you know from the moment they say 'hullo' if they are unduly excited or depressed.

This undisguised free-flow of sound reflects the instinctive, or informal use of the signals, and likely pre-dates the first word-cries uttered by man. For even if he could communicate by look and by touch he often had need, especially at night or in difficult terrain, to reinforce his message by sound. So his grunts, calls, and murmurs evolved into a first means of symbolizing his message. Then as intelligence developed, and as his voice alone could not make speech sounds, he made amazingly adaptive use of that part of his bone and muscle structure primarily created for breathing and eating.

Soon this new co-ordination led to the creating of word-sounds to indicate certain objects, probably still much accompanied by appropriate gesture, and the sounding of 'cave,' 'fire' or 'wild beast' would be reinforced by enactment of the image. With matters of survival often at stake this combination of the power of mind, heart and, because of the use of symbol, of imagination, behind the word-sound must have been intense; so, in the same cause, must have been the concentration of the listener.

The next miracle was the consensus of opinion that linked these isolated symbols of sound by a special system or grammar, which enabled formal language to open the way to new realms of understanding. Then came the development of different languages which still underline the essential needs by which a race survives. So that while in English, for example, there is one word for 'snow,' in Eskimo there are over twenty-four. Meanwhile, out of the need to record 'the hunt passed here' or 'that wild beast looked like this,' messages evolved into pictures and signs, and from a pictorial language into the symbols of written language. Through intricate use of space on stone, papyrus, or bark, man could now record ideas with permanence, and had the power of winging the exactitude of thought beyond generations and out into time.

Thus came the beginning of that long private transaction between the sound of speech and the silence of print – each, according to occasion, fulfilling a complementary but slightly different role of language. As the oral tradition was at the core of general education for millenia, including the legends and stories passed down by poets and balladeers – music again – so until now the written tradition has been at the core of formal education. For since Gutenberg and his movable type of the fifteenth century, when approximately a thousand books were published in a year, education invested in the one medium then capable of wide circulation of knowledge.

But now, with over a thousand books a day being published, plus the electronic proliferation of media through which information can be broadcast, the oral tradition has for the first time in centuries both the chance and the need to come back into its own. It is as if much of the emphasis on the written approach in education is changed not only by radio, films, computers, and television but also by that now simple gadget that lets every man hear, and record with permanence, his own or anyone else's speech. Indeed any instrument that records and projects voice and/or image tends to bypass the need to turn spoken signals into written signals.

All this is said to have had an impact on the way we speak today, for as Marshal McLuhan, guru of our communication age, noted in a recent address to the Canadian Speech Association: 'Gutenberg flattened the tune with silence; since then, with the honest exception of dialect which retains a way of life, it has been further deflated by the anonymity of a computerized society, bureaucratic living, and cultural counter-shock.' He also adds, 'modern society places a cultural impediment on emotional response in the voice.'

So as civilization develops, vocal signals, while still marvellously lively at times, have been adapted to suit the needs of various roles and occasions. In addition to using them to delineate meaning, as in raising the voice in query, or bringing it down in finality, formal use is influential in gaining a response. Thus there is the professional or business voice, designed to keep emotion out of the matter, such as the impersonality of the airline pilot who needs to use his p/a system almost solely in the interest of clarity. So impersonal is such use in some cases, however, that at airports and bus terminals the results, to uninitiated but needy passengers, are often unintelligible.

There is also the social voice, and here signals are so automatic that it is possible to say something verbally out of place provided that vocally the sound is as expected. In one experiment a girl arriving at a party was greeted by the hostess with the usual, 'How are you, my dear?' and passed happily down the line. But her actual reply was, 'I'm fine, thank you. I've just murdered my husband.'

Then there are the signals which reflect our personal idiosyncracies and which often come as a bit startling when people first hear a recording of their voice. 'Do I sound like that?' is often a two-fold response referring both to the quality of voice and to the signals underlying the speech. The first surprise is usually due to being accustomed to hearing the voice from inside, rather than from outside, ourselves. The second can be due to the flow of our signals being so automatically a part of ourselves that we do not always realize the impression they can give. Being human, we tend to wishful thinking and, even when genuinely interested in a subject, can be surprised if the voice seems to lack lustre, or if when we think we are being firm it comes over lacking in confidence, or over-confident when we don't mean it to.

These signals surround our daily, domestic, social, and working lives, and it is helpful to become aware of them and to listen through them to the core of what is being said. If we both let it and listen to it, the voice truly talks. And remember that this ancient, two-stringed instrument, with its resonating cavities and strange flaps on either side of the head, makes a more wonderful complement to the words and songs of all languages than any ever totally devised by man. Respect, nurture, and enjoy it.

Voice routine

Continue your routine as before, developing the variations on exercises for breathing, vocalized sighing, humming and vowel sounds. Continue by concentrating on one or two sets of consonants in conjunction with vowel sounds; add some work on articulation and projection; conclude with some reading aloud.

EXERCISES FOR EAR TRAINING
You have already been exercising a disciplined use of your ear in assessing what you want to achieve, and in evaluating initial progress during voice routine.

Specific exercises for ear training can include the finding of your middle note, as suggested in this chapter. Then, to increase familiarity with your range, begin work on combinations of notes. This should be done not merely to put your voice up or down artificially and from without, but to enable you to reflect the full potential of thought and feeling that lies within.

– Combine breathing with humming, on your middle note.
– Go one note down, and return.
– Go two, and then three, notes down; and return in the same order.
– Go three, and then four, notes down; and return in the same order.

It is often wise to space this development over a week or so, but when you can encompass the above easily on a breath, explore your upper range.

– Combine breathing with humming and, checking that there is a good
  buzz, go one note up and return.
– Go two, and then three, notes up; and return in the same order.
– Go three, and then four, notes up; and return in the same order.

If you are maintaining a sense of ease and forward placing, combine one note down and one up on a breath; two down and up, and eventually three and four down and up.

– Try to keep the sense of progression from one note to another as light
  and bubbly as you can.
– Over some months, repeat the above work on range, using your own
  combinations of vowels and consonants as in your previous routine.

MODULATION

Inflection
Initial work on gaining variety or modulating the voice can be done by returning to a good hum.

- When the hum is buzzing well, inflect it up: Mmmmmmmm ⟋
- Inflect it down: Mmmmmmm ⟍
- Experiment with a combination of both: Mmmmmmm ⟋⟍
- And the opposite: Mmmmmmmm ⟍⟋
- Listen to the variety of implication that can be given behind a glide.
- Decide on a mood you wish to imply, such as being enthusiastic or disappointed about something, and if working with a partner, see if he receives it.

A point that is easy to forget here is to be sure to start a glide at the opposite level to the required end. So during practice, begin on the lowest note you can comfortably manage if you want to go towards an upward, leave-it-in-air, finish. Conversely, start on the highest note you can accomplish without compression and caricature, if you are to come down in a clear statement of finish or conclusion.

Strange as making these vocal curlicues may sound in isolation, they can, in addition to providing awareness of potential range, pinpoint the occasional problem concerning monotony in the voice. This is not always a simple technical matter but, like the tortoise who keeps his head in the shell, can be related to a sense of vulnerability. But it is surprising how many people find that aiming for contrast helps clarify meaning; and to hear effective contrast played back on a tape-recorder gives new confidence.

Pitch
Begin to listen more acutely to the variation of pitch you can attain, and develop some of the notes explored in ear training during the flow of connected speech. For example, take Mary and her little lamb again, or what you will, and see if you can talk the first line on a high, middle, and low level respectively:

```
Mary had a little lamb ⎤
        Mary had a little lamb      ⎤
              Mary had a little lamb.      ⎤
```

- If you feel you are making a clear difference between them, and here use of your rough tape on the recorder can be illuminating, try the line on five different levels.
- Take your time and, if you wish, a breath between each, and think in advance of simply coming down five vocal steps:

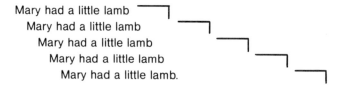

Mary had a little lamb
  Mary had a little lamb
    Mary had a little lamb
      Mary had a little lamb
        Mary had a little lamb.

Pace

One of the less obvious aspects of monotony which can be hard for the user to perceive unaided, is an unadventurous, slow pace. No matter how potentially interesting the content of material, the result can give an impression of lack of involvement. It may also narrow the pitch range, lead to repetitive inflections, and create a usually unintentional invitation to listen out. But where there's a will, such a pattern can be broken. It involves practice in speaking at different speeds, yet without either gabbling or unwinding the words like a relaxed spring.

- Try the whole four lines of Mary and her lamb again very lightly and quickly.
- Try them slowly and heavily.
- Then slowly, as if relaxing someone; and quickly, as if awakening them to good news.

If, on the other hand, a fast pace seems a habit, assess your rate of words per minute from a passage of reading aloud and from a taped piece of your usual rate of talking. Compare it to the average rate noted under 'Listening, thinking, and responding' in Chapter 15. Then try to become aware of a rate that considers the needs of your listeners, who would perhaps prefer to think along with you than to have to chase after you.

Pause

In everyday life there is usually a subtle but unconscious interaction between the way we change pace and the way we use a concomitant length of pause. But while much attention may be paid to the pauses, or stop-marks of punctuation, during use of the written word, less is usually given to the help punctuation can provide in delivery of the spoken word. Some suggestions are included in Chapter 12, on reading aloud.

Clear use of contrast in parenthesis, for example, can open channels of meaning between speaker and listener. This is usually conveyed by a rising inflection and sometimes a slight pause before the less important phrase. This is followed by a quicker pace and lower pitch during the phrase, leading to a rising inflection and another slight pause before returning to the previous pitch and pace. A useful example for practice will be found in the assignments for Chapter 13.

Volume

While most people intuitively adapt their voices, it is useful to check that volume is suited to the needs of an occasion. Pitch, for example, can have a marked influence, higher levels tending to take a loud volume, and lower levels a low volume. So, though the result is closely linked to the energy and breathing involved, listen to see whether the levels complement or override each other.

When the voice is helping to create a sense of atmosphere, and pitch and volume tend to be low, note that any vocal constriction leading to a half-whisper should be avoided. Under these circumstances this can be a mark of strain, or of attempting to push out a half-digested impression, rather than letting the voice mirror what is truly and imaginatively within. The Chorus from many plays provides excellent practice in creating atmosphere; look at his lines in Anouilh's play, *Antigone*, at Thornton Wilder's Stage Manager in *Our Town*, and in many of Shakespeare's plays, particularly the lines beginning 'Now entertain conjecture of a time/When creeping murmur and the pouring dark/Fills the wide vessel of the universe,' from *Henry V*, Act IV.

Finally, here is part of an evocative poem about the Mari Lwyd, or Grey Mare, which was a wooden horse's head carried into houses in Wales on the last night of the year. Groups of singers and poets challenged those within to a rhyming contest; if the rhymes could not be met they claimed entry for food and drink. In the Prologue there is talk of midnight as 'burning like a taper,' and of the Living hearing the Dead 'tapping at the panes.'

– Visualize the occasion before you start. Try to speak it with a sense of the underlying rhythm of the clock as being as important as all the other impressions. The poet thought extreme rhythmic regularity in speaking these words of such importance that in stage performances he suggested the speakers rehearse with the aid of a metronome.

Midnight. Midnight. Midnight. Midnight.
Hark at the hands of the clock.
What shudders free from the shroud so white
Stretched by the hands of the clock?
What is the sweat that springs in the hair?
Why do the knee-joints knock?
Bones of the night, in the naked air,
Knock, and you hear that knock.

Midnight. Midnight. Midnight. Midnight.
Hark at the hands of the clock.
A knock of the sands on the glass of the grave,
A knock on the sands of the shore,
A knock of the horse's head of the wave,
A beggar's knock on the door.
A knock of a moth on the pane of light,
In the beat of the blood a knock.
Midnight. Midnight. Midnight. Midnight.
Hark at the hands of the clock.

The sands in the glass, the shrinking sands,
And the picklock, picklock, picklock hands.

Midnight. Midnight. Midnight. Midnight.
Hark at the hands of the clock.

From *The Ballad of the Mari Lwyd*, Vernon Watkins

Part Two
Your Own Words

6
Words Public

Prelude

In Part I we considered the development of your speaking instrument, and began exercises designed to lubricate and free the voice. These should be continued as the basis for all coming assignments for, once in trim, the voice should be kept supple and ready for all speaking needs. As the dancer, singer, or athlete must keep the instrument limber, so should the speaker. Then the impulse of meaning and feeling, which lies behind the sounding of words, can be as true to intent as possible.

In Part II we will consider the generation and use of your own good words, balanced in Part III with a look at other people's words. Meanwhile, we will include a brief discussion of some of the differences between the written and spoken word. For, sadly, throughout our education many of us found marks and grades depended more on the one than the other.

As mentioned near the end of the last chapter, the invention of movable type in the fifteenth century, resulting in the expansion of literacy, in turn helped create pressures for universal education, and led to a gradual takeover of the oral by the written tradition. So today, while teachers still talk, as indeed they have to, and create response through question and discussion, students continue to do much of their learning by listening, by mostly silent reading, and by use of radio and television programmes, films, and video and audiotapes. Their major feedback to all this input tends to be through use of the written word in the form of the essay, the composition, the precis, and the business letter and, more recently, through check-marks on multiple-choice, computerized-answer tests. Such instruction tends to focus on the written word. This is fine for people who are gifted, as with an ability to draw easily or to play the piano by ear, who have a talent for the spoken word and a background and ease in establishing relationships. For others, the situation can lead to a void since, once outside the classroom, the spoken word takes precedence in our ability to communicate and so to function.

So the spoken word tends to be taken for granted during our formative years, as though it were an invisible, or fifth, limb. It is one, however, through which we utter, and so outer, ourselves, to others, as they to us; and we extend use of it at three major levels. We have one use of the spoken word at home, another as we interact with society, and a third which we use in the world of work. While countless books have been written on style or manner of expression in writing, few comments have been made on this variety of manner in speech.

There is the relaxed core of our being, and so of our utterance, as expressed at home. Here we understand others who are hopefully dear to us, and we are so accustomed to their total pattern of communication that we may respond to their smallest change of attitude and vocal signal. When the atmosphere is of content and trust, providing a benediction to our going out and coming in, the pulse of signals flows from tribal groans, grunts, and whoops to familiar sayings and every kind of talk.

But in society, without the close history of familial association, we need to communicate with greater clarity. While this extension of ourselves is barely noticeable among complete or long-term friends, we usually begin by making subtle adjustments to comparative strangers. What we say and how we say it are somewhat edited, as we adopt both vocabulary and style to their needs within the context of the situation.

In the world of work, including trade, business, the professions, and the arts, we need a more responsible use of the spoken word, which is often a vital factor in our everyday function and in matters affecting promotion and even survival. In the complexity of this world we may also need to adjust to different levels of an organization and to speak, as it were, up to our superiors, laterally to colleagues, and down to other employees. Ideally, this takes mutual respect and consideration for the relationships involved, and for the facts required and so, as mentioned in Chapter 1, for that essential quality of imagination.

Finally a consistency of this trilingualism, where there is no great divergence between one idiom and another, could be said to be one of the marks of a mature, integrated personality. But whether this quality is regarded as 'being the same to all people,' or simply as 'not putting on airs,' can depend on any pecking order, and on the good fortune of the relationships involved.

It is with the third level of utterance that we shall now be concerned; and because it can be tempting to place great reliance on written preparation alone, we will take a brief look at some of the differences between the written and the spoken word.

Some differences between the written and spoken word

The written word is a safe word, though like most forms of communication it is often tough to bring into being. It jogs the memory, is easy to retrieve (if we are tidy enough to know where we have put it or where else to find it), and can be exact, as there is usually time to think it out in advance.

The written word can be dwelt upon, and can then convey an intricate compression of ideas. The late novelist and dramatist Jean-Paul Sartre once noted in an interview that there is a tendency to confuse simplicity with style, which to him was a way of saying three or four things in one. While he did not preclude simplicity, he felt that the artist in language 'arranges words in such a way that according to the emphasis he puts on them, they can mean different things at different levels.'

The written word also provides a sense of control, of pre-thought ideas as suited as possible to a particular need, and can be refined, honed, and often cut to this end. In the case of the printed word it usually carries the advantage of advice, or the disadvantage of the occasional machinations, of an editor. This middleman between publisher and eventual reader can play a vital part in going through a manuscript for style, consistency, grammar, and relevance; and later we shall refer to the speaker's need to consider his own editing of the spoken word.

The written word is hopefully expressed in undisturbed privacy and concentration, and usually received in the same way. For example, have you ever tried to write or to read in the middle of a crowded room, when the radio or television are on, or when people interrupt your silent train of thought by talking to you?

But the spoken word requires instant commitment while in direct contact with others and during all the hurly-burly that can surround human interchange. There is, however, a fair chance that the better we use this primary means of expression, the better we may use the written word. Ideally, rather than seeing them as different factions, with one taking precedence, each should be seen as complementary and evolving out of harmony and understanding of the other.

An illustration of this was noted recently in an interview by the New Zealand Department of Education with Christabel Burniston, Director of the English Speaking Board (International). Mrs Burniston gave an example of where a Principal of a large new comprehensive school in the UK, shocked at the standard of oral communication from both pupils and teachers, abolished written exams for a year and made the teachers learn how to examine subjects orally. Consequently written work became relative, arising from realistic situations. The change was dramatic; the school became alive, vigorous, and enthusiastic and the results in external written examinations surpassed their previous records.

The spoken word is a volatile word. Speaking and listening to it requires a fast use of memory so that, until the advent of the tape recorder, memory was also the only means of referral or retrieval. As we shall discuss in Chapter 15 on listening, not only does the speaker attempt to pre-create and then remember what he is going to say, he also has to remember what he has just said. Otherwise he could become vacantly repetitious or wildly inconsistent.

While preparation for formal use should be just as careful as for the written word, actual delivery cannot wait upon mood, or delayed inspiration, or second thoughts. Any deliberation needs to be resolved in advance of expression. And because a listener cannot go back, unless a recorder has been used, it is essential that the ideas are kept to a simple progression and are simply presented. That is, they should be designed more for reception and retention through the microphone of the human ear than for the camera of the human eye. Thus some written material, such as the private intricacies of a masterly Virginia Woolf, or the compressed factual thought of much research, or a certain amount of modern poetry, is not always suited to be reclothed in the sound of the spoken word.

The spoken word creates an immediate and often very personal response. But however carefully thought out in advance, there is never any total guarantee of the impression it will have on a listener. It can require an adaptability on the part of the speaker, for which experience with mainly the written word can leave him unprepared. Yet response can generally be forecast by the purpose of the situation and the role concerned, and usually reflects the pecking order of those involved. For example, the speaker on a soapbox in London's Hyde Park Corner, or at a political meeting, can expect to be heckled, and the repartee and occasional wit are part of the fun and challenge of the situation. But the same behaviour would be unlikely to interrupt a management meeting.

Fundamentally, it is the relationships between people that form the underlying base of human interaction. In addition, all effective communication needs a sense of trust, and one of the ways in which this is indicated is through a sense of mutual respect. Here it is helpful to remember that communication is a factor that takes place as much inside the individual as outside. For, as counterpart to the link between what we wish to say and how we eventually express it, comes the important factor of a balancing trust and respect for our own selves. This element of a basic self-confidence, which does not have to be flamboyant, is a prerequisite of effective use of the spoken word. Otherwise, by setting up a virtual sound barrier to his own belief, self-doubt can defeat a speaker from within.

So it is best to prepare the spoken word with a positive concentration on what is to be said and to keep in the back of the mind the age-old advice, 'to thine own self be true' because *(a)* you haven't got time for anything else, and *(b)* your own integrity is the longest-running thread of your communicating life.

Voice routine

Continue as before, allowing time for preparation, relaxation, and a check of ease of movement and posture. Work on breathing and humming to help placing and resonance.

– Read the following lines silently a few times, letting the images and sensations come to you. When you can conjure echoes of the peace of the music, speak the lines with the same sense of absorption. Initially your voice may be so quiet that barely anyone else could hear it. But as long as it is free and neither breathy nor raspy, all is well; projection can come later.

There is sweet music here that softer falls
Than petals from blown roses on the grass,
Or night-dews on still waters between walls
Of shadowy granite, in a gleaming pass;
Music that gentlier on the spirit lies,
Than tired eyelids upon tired eyes;
Music that brings sweet sleep down from the blissful skies.

From *Song Of The Lotus Eaters*, Tennyson

– After a break and more deep, easy breathing, try the lines again a couple of times. Maintain your relaxed concentration, and as you let the voice become fuller, the sound waves will carry your intent.

When such lines are familiar to you, they can be useful to speak after your initial relaxation, before considering standing and posture.

Try to balance the content of your routine so that there is also time for patter exercises, for lightness and clarity. These should be preceded by matching and mixing work on vowels and consonants as previously suggested.

– Then try the transition into such as:

Of all the girls that are so smart
   There's none like pretty Sally;
She is the darling of my heart,
   And she lives in our alley.
There is no lady in the land
   Is half so sweet as Sally;
She is the darling of my heart,
   And she lives in our alley.

Of all the days that's in the week
   I dearly love but one day –
And that's the day that comes betwixt
   A Saturday and Monday;
For then I'm drest all in my best
   To walk abroad with Sally;
She is the darling of my heart,
   And she lives in our alley.

From *Sally In Our Alley*, Henry Carey

– Keep the lines light as if talking cheerfully to someone.
– As they become familiar, give them a swing of thought and breath so that you can say the first, and then the second, of each four lines on a breath.
– Do some reading aloud of your own choice.

7
Giving a Speech 1

A speech, to be effective, requires as much inner preparation and gathering of resources as does creative work in other arts. Through words, chosen to express carefully thought-out ideas, it must be shaped and fashioned into its own form, and then expressed with apparent ease through the medium of the speaker's voice and personality. Preparation includes as much, if not often more, than the gathering of every item for a model airplane enthusiast, or ingredients for a cook. It also requires the creation of a new design or recipe, as it were, from scratch. Like many other forms of seemingly easy creation, it can be as hard to bring the final material into being as to carve granite with the fingernails; yet the result should abide by the dictum, 'the height of art is to conceal art,' or 'hard to write, easy to read.'

Initially there are very few short-cuts, and even in the long run the form of preparation remains the same, although experience leads to ease in handling, shaping, and delivering the material. Fundamentally, eighty per cent of the key to success lies in the most thorough and careful preparation that time can allow. The same degree of care must then be passed on to the remaining twenty per cent. If this, which concerns delivery, is poor, it can negate otherwise excellent preparation.

An interesting example of this occurred in British parliamentary history in the late eighteenth century, when it is said that the playwright, Sheridan, also a good actor, heard a remarkable speech in connection with the trial of Warren Hastings. But the MP giving it stumbled so badly and was so boring that the House practically emptied. Sheridan, with his instinct for the spoken word, recognized the worth of the material and asked his colleague for a copy. Two weeks later the playwright gave the same speech – and sat down to a standing ovation.

When you know you have to give a speech it should be possible simply to follow the excellent ground rule of decide what you want to say, and then say it. While the thread of this lifeline should be a useful guide to relevance, such a decision is in itself an important landmark, and may not be reached until many factors have been mulled over. So allow plenty of time, and be prepared to use patience. Although no one can actually be taught to give a speech, any more than to write or to act, there are guidelines which can help in both preparation and delivery.

Start with the situation

The preparation of a speech should start with the full context of the situation in mind including:
1 The purpose of the occasion, indicating in turn the expectations of the audience.
2 Some facts about the audience, including an approximate number and, where helpful, an indication of previous knowledge and experience in the topic, the age of the audience, and the economic and community background.
3 If you are part of a conference or a series of any kind, enquire about the main theme, and about previous and forthcoming areas being covered.
4 Ask about the space in which you will speak – hall, auditorium, or room – and about any need of special facilities. You might require electric points, or outlets, for certain aids such as slide-projector or a tape recorder. Find out if you are likely to be asked to use a microphone and, if at all possible, arrange to see the space in advance. In lieu of this a photograph can be helpful, as familiarity with the situation can give extra confidence.
5 Settle any business arrangements in advance concerning expenses, travel and accommodation; and any fee. Be prepared to supply a photograph, usually a glossy print about twenty by twenty-five centimetres, and a brief biography for publicity purposes.
6 Double-check the date, time, and place of the occasion, being sure to keep an organizer's phone number handy, including area codes, in case of last-minute thoughts or emergencies.
7 Request a clear idea of the length of time you will be asked to speak, and whether there will be time for a question/discussion period afterwards.

During the preparatory period, be ready to put yourself in the place of your eventual audience. For if what you want to say takes a while in coming, remember it is likely to arise gradually out of a marriage of your topic to the needs of your audience.

Avoid any thought of your future audience as a potential enemy. It can be as easy to build dragons in a smoke as to create castles in the air. Remember that assumptions breed attitudes, and by assuming the audience will be friendly and interested you will bypass negative thoughts and conserve positive energy.

Be realistic. Remember that clarity of expression depends on clarity of intent. Often because of pressures of time we try to communicate before we have fully thought out what we are trying to say. Eventually the clarity must progress through the entire process of preparation and delivery, and so effective results fundamentally arise out of good organization.

Preparation of the speech

Whether you are going to give a speech lasting forty-five minutes to a large conference, or lasting ten minutes to other members of a class, your aim is the same: to communicate, as clearly as you can, the purpose that lies behind the medium of your words. While it is standard to point out that this will fall into one of the major categories of to inform, instruct, persuade, or entertain, it is also worth remembering that many effective speakers use a subtle blend of all these headings.

We will assume that you have chosen a topic and your main purpose is clear. But if, by the way, choice is ever a problem, always try to speak about something that you know and/or have considerable interest in, and in which you have some opportunity for research. Let us take a countdown of points that can assist in the preparation of any kind and length of speech, always bearing in mind that as experience develops you can quicken and vary such an approach enormously.

THINK
Be prepared to start your own think-tank. If you are speaking on a topic that is totally familiar to you, it is unlikely that at this stage you would have to do much more than to select and organize your points into an order that would be most helpful, and interesting, to your audience. In which case you may care to move straight on to points about practice under the heading: Practice of delivery. But if your material is not yet pre-thought it will need fashioning and bringing together out of your knowledge and resources; be ready to exercise patience, for initially a speech is as unlikely to come pre-cut into mind as is the complete material for a story or an article.

The material for your think-tank is simply a blank piece of paper, preferably a distinctive colour so that it will not easily be lost. Over a period of some days, weeks, and occasionally months, take time to jot down any ideas, sources, references, and queries that you might need to follow up. Remember your resources may finally be gathered through libraries and museums, art galleries and science or theatre organizations, specially heard or remembered programmes on radio or television, and occasionally through your own, and possibly recorded, interviews of other people.

Meanwhile some order of progression may come easily to mind, and if so, on another blank page, print your major headings. Cross off items on the first page as you fit them within the appropriate section on the second page.

But if the total content, let alone the progression, is uncertain for a while, keep plugging away at jotting down any and every kind of relevant idea. If you can leave a gap of a few days you may then take a new look at this material, and out of it will find certain topics that can be grouped together. Classify, and then mark them under As, Bs, Cs, Ds, or however many major topics you have. But remember to be realistic, and try to keep your potential material within reasonable bounds for the time-span of your speech. For example, one major heading may be enough for ten minutes, and three to five for forty minutes. Always bear in mind the need to avoid literary complexities of expression even in your notes, as these may be useful within the context of the written medium, but can overburden the spoken word and be indigestible to the listening ear.

ORGANIZE AND SYNTHESIZE

So you now have headings on the second page and have crossed off appropriate notes as you transfer them from the first page. Out of this process two things can happen relating to the order of your material:

1 As you would try out places for the fit of different pieces in a jigsaw puzzle, you may want to re-fit certain points under different headings.

2 You may re-order points under the same headings, so that what started as section C is seen as being best near the beginning of your speech and is now reclassified as section A, while section B contains major points helpful near the end and may be reclassified as section C.

Thus the preparation of a speech is a complex process and usually the opposite of the Alice-in-Wonderland advice to 'begin at the beginning and go on until you come to the end'; so you may want to formulate the conclusion first. This, presumably, is to be the target and to include the primary purpose of your speech, so all other points should lead logically to it. Similarly, to cap all, it is often best to work on the introduction last; always try to think of a lead-in that will hook interest.

So you now have a body of ordered material, and you know where it is to lead and roughly how it is to start. But take a long, hard look at it in relation to relevance and suitability and, in lieu of an editor, put yourself in the place of the audience and be prepared to pare away. Ask yourself if these points express what you really want to say and if they will meet the needs of your listeners. What sort of questions are likely to be asked? Can you fill any such gaps, or will you deliberately leave points that might create inquiry? Have you got your facts right, sources available, quotes correct, and any difficult names or words practised for easy delivery?

At some point – when is up to you and largely dependent on how the material is shaping up – one of two things is likely to happen. Either you will have too little material, or if you have been doing your homework well, too much. Here is the time to synthesize, to be sure to include your major points and to be prepared to sacrifice minor points. This part of your preparation will help ensure that your speech is relevant, and enable you to clarify the result through developing the art of making anything complex sound simple.

WRITE IF NECESSARY, BUT ALWAYS REDUCE TO NOTES

You now have a second or possibly third draft, or more, of well-ordered headings, possibly some sub-headings and detailed notes on a page. There are two choices ahead: if you feel confident in the flow of ideas, you can neaten your notes and start to practise your speech aloud; or you can take a great deal more time and write your speech out – but then, unless the occasion is very formal and makes particular demands, it is essential that you re-reduce it to notes and do not merely leave it in written-out form.

If you choose the latter course, bear in mind that the purpose is to give you a chance to find out exactly what you want to say in detail – so 'outering' it from yourself through the written medium. Avoid, however, any thought of memorizing it, or leaving it in written-out form so that you can partly, or sort of vaguely, read it. As just mentioned, there are a few occasions when an expression needs to be set down and followed implicitly, such as a eulogy or a special presentation; and indeed there are times when particularly busy people, having supplied the gist, have their speeches written for them. But ideas for this different need will come in a later chapter on reading aloud.

Remember, when you are preparing a speech, that you are going to give your material through the public medium of speaking rather than the private medium of writing, and we have already discussed some of the differences between them. Everyday speaking carries a sense of a direct form of flow from which, without artificiality, public speaking should simply be an extension. The process of writing, in a sense being slower, tends to be more formal and thought out. This can make for a stilted delivery, which seems to take little notice of the audience. Such delivery can be due to poor reading, but can also hinge on the vital factor of a degree of spontaneity in the air when notes, rather than exactly pre-formed material, are used. Even the speaker does not then know exactly what form the expression of his ideas will take. This makes him re-think the impulse behind them, and join them and otherwise custom-tailor them for the particular needs of the audience and the occasion. So by all means write your speech in advance; but prepare to live dangerously, face your audience, and speak directly to them with cues from your notes. You may surprise yourself, for the freedom gained is enormous.

Everybody has their own method of making and using notes, varying from small cards placed carefully in order with a section of information on each, on one side only; to headings, cue ideas, and any special quotes on one side of a piece of paper. During your practice you will learn to use whichever method you find easiest on a glance-down and scoop-up basis; accepted in this fashion, the audience will barely notice your notes, and the flow of your speech will run with a sense of control and ease. Be sure to prepare the notes with maximum legibility, using a clear scale in terms of headings and sub-headings, grouping each section in a surround of space.

A factor which you will have considered in planning your material is length, and it is useful to incorporate some account of this within your notes. It is usually reckoned that we speak at an average rate of 125 words per minute, and since you may want to ease this to allow for your audience to adapt to your personality and to think over what you have to say, you could consider a delivery of about 120 words per minute. Thus a 20-minute speech would require around 2,400 words, a 30-minute speech, 3,600 words and a 40-minute speech, 4,800 words, or the length of a sizeable article, which would often be expected to take some weeks to prepare. So note-wise, it can be useful to include time-signals indicating the amount of material you plan to cover in, say, each sixth of your speech. This will help ensure that you keep your introduction in proportion, give the fullest time to the body of the speech, and have sufficient time for the conclusion. You may also want to work in a few places where it would be helpful to take a brief review of what has been said, and to indicate what is to come.

Having gathered your resources, formed and refined your material a number of times, and begun to complete the first eighty per cent of your preparation, you are ready for the final twenty per cent, which concerns delivery. It is now essential that you allow, and indeed make, time for practice aloud.

PRACTICE OF DELIVERY
It is surprising how often the delivery of a speech has a 'stale, flat and unprofitable' and inaudible air because the speaker assumes that preparation

stops at the stage of written notes. But here is the moment to borrow a variation out of the typist's notebook, for truly 'Now is the time for all good sound to come to the aid of the party,' since all those good words, signifying much thought, may lack impact for an audience without practice in being well spoken. If it is any comfort, countless famous figures throughout history, from Demosthenes to Churchill, have gone through rigorous periods of such time well spent. Granted actual experience is of the greatest help, but now must come that fine tuning of words which will give you the best possible chance of control during delivery. For then you will need an extra awareness for establishing a rapport with your audience, and you can make room for this if you have planned to some degree not only what you are going to say, but how you are going to say it.

First take a few runs at the whole. Familiarize yourself with the development and, above all, with the continuity of your material.

Make one golden rule: keep thinking ahead. Understandably, because the pace of preparation is slow, and you are suddenly using your material at the rate of one-hundred-and-something words per minute, this will happen unevenly at first. Make a habit of giving some additional pause between headings to collect the subsequent thoughts; and, if you find occasionally that speaking catches up with thinking, deliberately use a short pause, break step and re-group.

After two or three initial runs you will soon be encouraged to find how well you know the material.

Try to forget any sense of feeling foolish because you appear to be talking to yourself. Naturally, with an audience it will sound different, as communication is a chain and without that link you are, temporarily, speaking in a void. If it helps, address a pet dog, cat, or canary – even a sleeping one – as their very presence will give you a slight edge towards the outering of your ideas.

Remember that speaking in public is simply an extension of your everyday utterance and not a matter of putting on artificialities of voice and pronunciation. But, because it is to be extended for reception and full understanding by a number of people at once, it must to that degree be enlarged; and that enlargement must carry your message clear in sound and in meaning. So, according to the size of the room or hall, you will need to adapt projection, and modulation and to be and look relaxed and in confident control of the situation. This is where regular practice of your voice routine begins to pay results. At some point you might also try speaking in a space similar in size to the one in which you will give your speech.

Now that continuity is coming, consciously experiment during one or two runs at different forms of wording. Your notes are only a blueprint, so be able and ready to change and adapt the expression of ideas as you go. Sometimes illustration by a brief personal anecdote here, or reference to a public figure there, may help to enliven your speech. It may also give you a sense of confidence and control in using brief examples of extemporaneous material.

But above all, remember a further intrinsic difference between the written words involved in your preparation and the spoken words of your delivery: the written word is largely interpreted through the mind of the reader, the spoken word through the voice of the speaker. It is up to you, therefore, to comment on your material. A speech that is to be effective cannot be delivered passively; all those good words possess neither life nor meaning for others unless you breathe into them a clear echo of your original impulse in forming them.

So now is the time to decide where you need points of emphasis or degrees of contrast which might be indicated by changing the pace or lowering or raising the pitch in comparison to a previous section. In some cases, mark in the need for a special breath because you have a long haul of a quote coming; or in others, mark where a pause will show something important is about to be said, or that you are moving to another heading.

Naturally these oral comments cannot be done artificially, and it will be found that emphasis, for example, sounds immature if merely conveyed through stress or weight on words or phrases. It will usually be found that this is best conveyed by a sure but subtle use of all the factors mentioned above. Here again, the voice routine, having kept things in trim, will enable you to exercise the varying degrees of subtlety you now need. Interpretation must be true to impulse, and if concentration is complete the voice will mirror intent.

Finally it is worth while considering making a tape-recording of what is now a full draft of your speech. Try to avoid any stopping and starting, but take a complete run-through to solidify continuity and timing. Playback will indicate very quickly whether you are achieving the life and variety of your aims.

Making a tape will also accustom you to possible use of a microphone during delivery, and management of this factor can become an art in itself. The advantage, however, is that you can address a large number of people while speaking comparatively quietly. Instead of using energy to project, it can be channelled into clarity of thinking and appropriate variety in the voice. So speak quietly, and within fifteen to thirty centimetres of the mike. It is important to remember that this approximate distance must be maintained even when addressing people sitting at the side of the room or hall; and it is still just as important to share and project visual impressions of face, posture, and any gesture. All of which, interestingly enough, has perhaps come so under the influence of the mike that, in comparison with recordings and films of politicians of the 'twenties and 'thirties, it is as if recent generations have tended to become expressionless. While there may be many reasons for over-naturalism, it gives us cause to wonder whether the sheer proliferation of media does not at times negate the message ...

However, if you are to be faced with a microphone, practise its effective use. But if you have choice in the matter and feel you can project in the space provided, better do your own thing and reach your audience through the microphone of your own resonance; they will probably bless you for it. Why use an aid when you can reach people direct? And the more direct your communication, the more effective your speech.

Voice routine

Continue as before, trying to keep to a schedule of fifteen to twenty minutes every day, or thirty minutes every other day.

– Following exercises for humming, resonance and projection, read the following lines a few times silently, letting them flow through you. When ready, speak them quietly and gently. You do not have to 'do' anything with them, but using the impetus of the rhythm, think of releasing their spirit with your breath.

Fear no more the heat o' the sun,
　　Nor the furious winter's rages;
Thou thy worldly task hast done,
　　Home art gone, and ta'en thy wages;
Golden lads and girls all must,
　　As chimney-sweepers, come to dust.　　From *Cymbeline*, Shakespeare

An assignment

Prepare your ideas for a short, eight-to-ten-minute speech on a topic that will have a vivid memory for you. Choose your own, letting it follow the useful axiom: speak about what you know. If you would like an idea, consider my first: day at work; trip overseas; car, bike, or home.

– Decide whether your major purpose is to inform, entertain or what-have-you. Once you have thought it over, you will probably find more material than you can encase within the few minutes required.

– Remember this preparation is part of the important discipline of being able to cut, pare, and synthesize.
– Come to the nub of the experience without taking up too much time on the introduction.
– Avoid any sign-off that fades into a '... and, er – that's all ...' Finish with a firm, easy conclusion.

8
Giving a Speech 2

Nerves

The question of how to deal with nerves is an understandable anxiety felt in varying degree by all whose function requires that they communicate in public. Fortunately the challenge of the situation usually becomes a saving grace, which brings out the best in the speaker; in fact, some people thrive and do splendidly while skating upon what to others is very thin ice.

Since it can be helpful to take out a problem, dust it off and look at it from a few sides, rather than go straight for possible antidotes, we may agree that the greatest bogey is fear, which takes many forms, any or all of which can make an otherwise happily functioning individual pray for deliverance by a fast opening of the earth. To the inexperienced, the fear is often simply of the unknown, for the role and function of the speaker is momentarily that of a leader, or of an explorer. This requires a public commitment and the ability to turn other people's minds, and occasionally their hearts, to some type of action. To be an instigator can lie hard with those who are unaccustomed to taking this kind of initiative.

Then there is fear of failing, which may be a compound of personal expectations coupled with assumptions about what other people think. It is tempting in this to create a mountain of vulnerability and to see it leading to negative comment on appearance, or grooming, or voice and general mannerisms – apart from the mere content of the speech. Yet all these are aspects of our individuality which each of us carries about more or less cheerfully every single day. But possibly the worst fear is that of loss of words. This can be a dreaded personal experience and one, it is felt, that will cause the speaker to seem foolish.

Whatever the fear, it tends to manifest itself in various kinds of tension, resulting in a negative use of time, resources and energy; and all too often for no better reason than a lack of positive aims to replace negative attitudes. These set up blocks and tend to become to the speaker what writer's block is to the writer: an interruption to the flow of communication. But where the writer bemoans privately, the speaker has to face his problems instantaneously and publicly, and may try to resolve them by either of the age-old responses of fight or flight.

The first response can lead to a pattern of get-it-over-quick, and so of speaking much faster and, because of hardly daring to take notice of the audience, giving an impression almost of belligerence. At another extreme it can lead to a pattern of continue-to-talk-at-all-costs and a repetition of points, as if the speaker is lost in waves of words, leading to a kind of verbal overkill. The flight response shows in other ways that the speaker does not want to be there. A sense of discomfort may be conveyed by a sad, dismal tone. The result, often called speaking in a minor key, lacks variety and can sound bored. Another symptom of reluctance for the occasion may be conveyed by general reticence. This usually takes the form of an over-economy and brevity which quickly becomes mirrored in uncertainty in the voice, and in everyday terms is called shyness. It can be interrupted by hesitant pauses and often by the verbal whiskers of 'um,' 'sort of,' and 'y'know' and may lapse into an unhappy inaudibility.

The need for flight may also set up such barriers that the speaker does, in a sense, freeze; the body remaining rooted while the mind shuts off, leading to the chasm of a loss of words and so of ability to continue. All of which may be accompanied by shivers in the voice, due to tense breathing, and to tremors in the body – somehow most awful if behind the knees, because the whole posture is affected.

So much for the worst.

It is hopefully obvious, however, that none of the above need occur if the speaker is well prepared, and we will deal with the derivative need of speaking extemporaneously, following a brief look at other special occasions. But it is also helpful to realize that any form of speaking in public is a test, and that speakers react differently to the edge of anticipation and to trying to achieve the best expression of their material during the time available.

Antidotes to nerves

Look good. Be as well groomed as you can and wear something suitable but comfortable.

Forget about yourself. It may be cold comfort but your audience does not know what is coming and is far more interested in your message than in your nerves. Many inexperienced speakers are cheered to find after their trial runs that no one in the audience noticed their attack of nerves.

Your function is to join your audience to your material and as soon as you outer, or extend, yourself for them, and control the thread of your material, your personality will aid and abet your cause. Keep your concentration outwards, your thoughts ahead, and let the extension occur naturally, while making the occasion as interesting as you can.

Here some people feel that they are naturally reticent and don't want to what they call 'act,' and become something they are not. While this need not be if the speaking is truly an extension of the self, such a view can also indicate a confusion of roles, or purpose. Granted the speaker requires facets of the actor's art, such as the ability to share thoughts and feelings in the presence of a large number of people, and that this needs an affinity for the tools of language and a flexibility of voice and manner in the service of the material. But the actor faces a different challenge in that having studied the impulse behind someone else's words, he then becomes someone other than he is, giving a total impression of seeing the world from behind, as it were, the eyes and heart of another human being.

The public speaker always remains himself and does not require this particular form of illusion; though he may convey illusion through taking the audience out of their particular space and time by the evocative use of his own words and occasionally, as during an anecdote, by dramatizing a situation.

But no matter to what extent a speaker feels trepidation in advance, solid preparation and careful practice will see him over what can be the hump of the first thirty seconds. From then on there will be a familiar sense of knowing the material from within the bone. This will come from the process of previous thought and organization and also from the interesting fact that one of the best ways to learn material is to speak it out loud. This need not imply the old-fashioned learning by rote of set material, but rather that we learn by constant reformulation of thought and by the actual sounding, and thus hearing, of it from within our own being.

Naturally audience response has a considerable effect on a speaker, and where totally positive it is one of the best antidotes to nerves that anyone can request. They may simply disappear and a splendid time may be had by all.

But there are times when 'all occasions do inform against me,' when an audience can convey a stolid, 'tell me something, damn you' look, and this is where, if necessary, they must be worked upon and literally wooed by a subtle adaptation of content and delivery. If it becomes obvious, however, that they don't wish to budge, and you have tried your best, don't kill yourself. Your energy may be better received another day; deliver your material as clearly as you can, and it may yet have significance for some.

There is a final hazard which can at some time plague any speaker, and this is the thudding discovery that those precious notes have been lost or mislaid. Even the ultimate nightmare has, however, a solution. Concentrate on the basic structure of your speech, and you may find it is more firmly in your mind than you imagined. If your preparation has been thorough you can become surprisingly independent of your notes, and while you may forget a few points you can acquit yourself well. Or remember the ancient Chinese proverb, 'When defeat seems inevitable – relax and enjoy it.'

Delivery

Arrive in good time and with your notes and any aids, such as slides for a projector, in good order.

Quietly gather concentration, relax, keep in mind how you are going to begin, and do a quick revision of the main threads of your material.

Listen to any introduction given you, and be prepared to sidestep for a moment and refer to it. A quick comment, small anecdote, or touch of humour can deflate what could otherwise be a somewhat formal atmosphere. A brief laugh also serves to unite an audience, giving you a useful stepping-stone into relating with them and so joining them to the business in hand.

Then let everyone settle.

And pause. Allow yourself to breathe.

This five-second moment of silence following stillness is one of the world's best signals for creating expectancy. It is similar to the taps used by a conductor, and the hush as the lights fade and as the curtain rises before a play. It will help calm any residue of nerves and make a fleeting but good impression that you are in control of the situation. This brief wait will produce a particular kind of quiet, and once you have created it, you possess a first boost to your morale.

Begin on a pitch slightly higher than medium, which will attract attention. Be sure of your mode of address, which you may need to check with your chairman in advance. Otherwise follow the style used in the preamble to the meeting, noting whether you are simply talking to 'Ladies and gentlemen' or to 'Ms President' or to the chairperson before going on to 'members of the such and such club.'

Take your time, talking with, not at, people, while thinking through the thoughts behind your notes and remembering to establish some eye-contact at various points in the room. Otherwise, when not scooping up notes, let your eyes maintain a look out at about their own level, neither wandering up to the ceiling nor down to the floor. They will reflect some part of your expression, so find a happy medium between the fact that while people do not want to be glared at, neither do they want to be ignored.

Keep an eye on your timetable, connecting with a handy watch by your notes, and if necessary stretch or condense some points as you go.

Remember that, having done your homework well, there is no need to interpolate excuses. The 'don't-hit-me-I'm-down' syndrome may intend to disarm, but more likely signals a cover-up.

Unless using it tongue-in-cheek, avoid lapsing into jargon which is a muddle of meaning lacking true sound.

Maintain your interest and enthusiasm in the subject. Where necessary, visualize what you are talking about and use total recall when recapturing experience. Remember that while you know what is coming your audience does not, and while you always assume they are interested they will be specially so if you give your material a first-time, first-thought quality of spontaneity.

Keep a weather eye out for audience reaction. Are their eyes open? Are some restless or chattery? Are they leaning forward or back? Nodding in occasional agreement with you? Looking generally happy about what they are hearing? Do different expressions skim their faces while concentrating on different aspects of your speech?

Be prepared not only to observe response, but to act upon it. As one speaker suggests, develop a feel for your audience so that you almost listen to them think. A change of pace and pitch, with some 'wake up' notes in the voice can help change a somewhat listless atmosphere; while if there has been a happy response to humour, take a pause, beginning again just before the laugh dies; or take quite a break if turning to a more serious heading.

When dealing with facts or making a careful point, it can be helpful not to hurry; you do not want to give verbal indigestion, so try a small slogan from an old Danny Kaye film. Playing a court jester, he was always anxious to know that his king got the message, and before moving on would inquire (which you can think silently rather than aloud) 'Get it? Got it? – Good.'

An audience likes to know when you are coming to an end. (Perhaps, as in a good play, to hang on to moments and to try to implant them in memory, or perhaps to summon a final spurt of concentration.) So signal by word and by voice that this is a final heading or point, or whatever; and then avoid any flattening or fading of the voice. Final impressions can be as important as first ones, so aim to wrap up your material; it does not have to be a flourish, but it does require a sense of finish.

If you want a parallel tune for practice, bear in mind the age-old story about the couple 'who lived happily ever after.' Give 'happily' an upward lift and slight pause, and you can give a nice wallop to 'after,' and you will sound as if you believe the words. But allow them to falter, or worse still, let 'ever after' lift upwards, and you could create some doubt about the couple's future.

Similarly if you try a phrase such as 'here endeth the lesson' and the signal fades upwards, it would seem to go against the words and the listeners would receive a miscue. But try the final word with a downward emphasis and you would gain a clearer effect.

So your good words are over; but rest assured that no matter how enthusiastic the comments, you will be able to think back to bits you feel could have gone better. And all the careful preparation in the world still needs to connect with your ability to work at building a relationship with your audience. Theory and advice can help clear the channels, but experience is the true mentor.

If your speech has required any form of demonstration or use of media, be sure to check the return of any hardware carefully. Likewise tidy your notes, which you may need again or may wish to use for reference and record.

Now that we have expanded ideas on giving a speech, we can condense the same principles for shorter but still public occasions, including introducing and thanking a speaker, or the sudden challenge of being invited to say a few words.

Brief words

Brief words, whether written or spoken, can be more challenging than longer compositions, for they allow no time for exposition or for warming to the material. The words must contain the nub of the thought, and to do this requires absolute economy, while the delivery has to sound easy. When there is opportunity for some preparation, it can be interesting to bear in mind a famous postscript in the correspondence of Count Metternich in the mid-nineteenth, and granted more verbose, century: 'Forgive me for the length of my letter as I have not had the time to be short.'

There is not room in a text of this coverage to deal with all the specialized needs of brief words, such as a toast to the bride or a presentation on retirement, which may be found in books dealing specifically with public speaking. We will, however, touch on one which may be mostly prepared, and one that may be partly prepared, and a third which may have to be completely spontaneous.

INTRODUCTIONS

When introducing a speaker to a group your purpose is clearly indicated by your function. And, in a sense, you are a surrogate for the speaker, who will probably have supplied a brief autobiography, but who can less comfortably and objectively talk about his or her own achievements.

- Aim to join the guest to the occasion.
- Be accurate in name and in pronunciation.
- Give a relevant, two-to-three-minute background on the speaker.
- Gather this from material you have asked the speaker to supply, rather than from what may be well-meaning friends or colleagues.
- Prepare these few minutes carefully. Write out your material if you feel the need of a precautionary lifeline. But do not leave it at that and memorize it, or even read an introduction. Always remember to reduce your speech to notes, and to deliver it from these reminders of the major headings.
- If you have time, aim to tell a simple anecdote as this can reveal more about the speaker as a human being than any number of facts about accomplishments.
- Try to weave in some humour, as this can give an early sense of proportion to the speaker and to the occasion.

Have a good beginning, which will hook, or sharpen interest, and know the final words you will use at the end. But let the body of your introduction avoid over-emphasis on the marvellous effect the speaker is going to have. By all means show support for him and for his cause, but let his words speak for themselves. Commendation and praise for his material can come from the person proposing a vote of thanks, and can be directly related to what he has then said.

Sound cheerful, optimistic, and awake. It is twice as hard for a speaker to pick up an audience if the introduction is in any way automatic, or reluctant, or doleful.

Again – be brief. Digest the horror story of the introduction that lasted forty-five minutes, when the speaker did the only thing possible – stood up, said 'Thank you,' and sat down.

THANKS

The simple function of saying 'Thank you' is a small art in itself. It should relate to what has been said and mirror the response of the audience, who would otherwise probably want to thank the speaker individually.

Whether as representative of a small or large group, it is important to be able to turn phrases of appreciation with grace and goodwill. It is particularly effective when, by referring to points and phrases used by the speaker, it shows you have paid the compliment of careful listening.

Again be brief. Having heard an effective speech or talk it would be inconsiderate to try and compete with it or copy it in any way, and two to three minutes is more than ample.

It is up to you to give the occasion a completing note in the voice. A sound that peters out at this point could be as inconclusive as the cast of a play taking a curtain call which looks uncertain, unsure, and unrehearsed. Remember that not only what you say but how you say it builds to a final note of appreciation by the audience, which they may want to accompany by a note of applause.

SAYING A FEW WORDS

Remember that the principles behind saying a few, or a few more, words are the same; to decide what you have to say and to communicate it as simply and clearly as possible. And the motions remain the same, though they are a compressed version of the preparation needed for a full speech.

If you get up to ten to fifteen minutes notice that you are to be called upon, you may want to jot down a few brief notes to keep you on track.

But however little notice is given, take a few seconds to relax, draw your resources together, and think clearly. Always try to let thought out as from a full vessel rather than squeeze it as from an empty tube. Consider quickly but carefully what is wanted to suit the occasion. Remember that your particular background is individual and that you will surface with three to five minutes or more of material that, within a general pattern, is unique to you. Aim for your own standards, avoiding the trap of feeling that there must be a certain model which, if you could but follow, would answer such needs; negative gropings take energy and concentration from the development of positive ideas.

Give yourself as much practice as possible in bringing thought into words while in the presence of other people. This is a process that occurs constantly in everyday life, except that now you will be looked at and listened to with greater expectation. Practising the assignments in this book, if possible in company with other people, and with occasional use of a tape recorder, will help set you on your way.

Even if you have time for little else, aim for two lifelines: how to begin and how to end. Then relax and sound confident.

In the next chapter we will turn from individual delivery of the spoken word to a means of exchanging ideas which has, with the rise of the media, become a popular way of expressing an opinion without requiring the same amount of formal preparation on the part of the guest, or main speaker. The interview format is being increasingly used by politicians, industrialists, conservationists, unionists, and artists – indeed by anyone with a cause – to expound their views. While ostensibly conducted in private within the walls of a television studio, or of an office, factory, or living room, it makes a useful contribution to our look at 'words public.' For these good words spoken in the form of apparently private conversation are actually intended for the widest possible public consumption.

Voice routine

Continue as before, then aim for the fun of the following lines, which can zip along like a polka:

> When I was a lad of twenty,
> And working in the High St Ken,
> I made quite a pile in a very little while –
> I was a bustle-maker then.
> Then there was work in plenty,
> And I was a thriving man,
> But things have decayed in the bustle-making trade
> Since the bustle-making trade began.
> From *I was a Bustle Maker Once, Girls*, Patrick Barrington

– Whisper the lines once or twice, to check clarity. Play with them and juggle with them. If in a group, take them through a couple of times so that each voice has two lines. Keeping the continuity in passing from one voice to another can help with flexibility and awareness.
– When this comes easily, try passing on one line each.
– Another time, check co-ordination of breathing with the swing of the rhythm, and you will probably be able to do four lines on a breath.
– Keep it light and bright, and think of setting toes tapping in response.

Assignments

Here we return to your first 8- to 10-minute speech.

- As D-day approaches, if preparation has been going well and you have practised the continuity out loud, make a rough tape.
- Listen to the playback positively, looking for the strengths as well as recognizing sections that need more work.
- If the transitions from one point to another, for example, are a little sticky, see if the hesitancy is due to the material or to your selection, or if you have not quite established a reminder of the underlying connections.
- Try to put yourself in the place of a listener and see if the order and development are clear.
- Remember that your aim is to share your experience as fully as possible in the time available.

Continue to widen the challenge and increase the range of your topics. List ideas for future use. Increase your time-span, and as you develop confidence in using your own words to communicate with others, add new material to your master tape.

- If in groups, write out headings for brief words, put them into a bag or box, and let everyone take a random choice.
- Speak sometimes with a few minutes' preparation, and sometimes extemporaneously.
- Remember that the more you exercise the muscles of communication, the more flexible and useful they will become.

9

Interviews on Radio and Television

The word interview has many connotations, ranging from the usually private selection of applicants for a job, to a means of bringing a person or event into public focus on radio or television. We will discuss the word in relation to the job interview later in the next chapter, but whatever the occasion, the purpose is to elicit and to give information. In either case it is important that, since much can hinge on content and impression, both question and answer are relevant, fair and well phrased and spoken.

The role of radio or television interviewer is unlikely to come to more than a few of us, and not everyone is likely to be an interviewee, or guest. But nobody knows when an invitation might come and, if the opportunity does arise the effect can be far-reaching. The format is also useful for our purpose of developing ease in communicating through the spoken word, and lends itself to practice through interesting assignments.

There is, however, another reason for a careful look at the media interview within the context of good words, well spoken. The situation is not only one that is familiar to us as onlookers, but it hinges on one of the most important skills in our communicating lives. This is the often prepared, but occasionally intuitive, ability to ask the right question in the right way at the right moment – a tall order, in which nobody succeeds all the time.

Furthermore, the formation of a question largely dictates the knowledge we receive, for by its very nature it tends to control the parameters of the answer. The question is not only a means of finding out for ourselves, or clarifying the opinions of others, or developing a further understanding of a situation; it also becomes a means of joining two or more sets of knowledge before proceeding further. Asking the right question can not only be pivotal to the countless forms of negotiation which enable us to advance through life, but it is often earmarked as the deciding factor behind the inspiration that has led to many great inventions.

Questioning is so universal to countless areas of our lives that its use is sometimes almost automatic; modes of greeting vary from 'how are you?' to 'hullo' to 'hiya' or 'hi' in such a way that they are now more signals for establishing contact than for seeking detailed answers. Among the first things we consider when buying something is the question 'how much?' And a more gentle art of questioning is, as we shall find, particularly helpful when we come to discuss making contact under the heading, 'words social.'

On another level, the questioning involved in a media interview provides a useful device for sharing information with a wide public without the problems of some alternatives. These could involve someone merely talking at the microphone or camera which, for lack of an exchange of ideas with another person, can become visually or vocally static. The radio talk or television address is an art in itself, involving most careful preparation of content, timing, and sheer speakability, and usually needs the fine honing of rehearsal, re-writes, and re-rehearsal. For most people such requirements would often be out of their range of experience, and the planning out of proportion to the time taken up by an interview. As we shall find, however, the informality set by the interviewer actually requires a disciplined technique to conform to the invisible demands of time versus content. For time is to broadcasting what space is to newsprint: limited and exact.

The guest

People are usually invited to be interviewed on something they know something about. But it is always wise to ask for clarification of a few details in advance, such as the type of programme, the main purpose of your interview as seen from the producer's viewpoint, and the amount of airtime involved.

Then have a think about it. If the appointment is for some days ahead, try and catch a sample of the programme so that you have some idea of the flavour and the personality of the interviewer in advance, and some assessment of the audience. Take a broad look at the type of questions you might be asked, and consider these along with the information you feel it would be helpful and interesting to give. Occasionally it is useful to have some additional ideas ready on which you might ask to be questioned. Arrive in good time, ready for a warm-up discussion.

Realize that you can't fully control the situation, but that you can, by some preparation and quick thinking, turn it to advantage if it does not move in the direction you want.

Be a good listener, but ready and able to take the initiative, or the melody, if you like, of the conversation. If the question is not clear, or is over-involved, ask for clarification.

Be ready to be spontaneous, and occasionally to go off on a surprise path. It is a rare interview that contains only what was expected, and few interviews include all that was intended.

Be perceptive about the format of the show and tailor your answers accordingly. If it is an in-depth, serious approach to a subject on which you are an expert, be prepared to give, and explain, some background information. An increasing number of media interviews are, however, part of entertainment programmes; in which case, be prepared to be reasonably light-hearted about the subject, but use the opportunity to slide in something worthwhile.

Because there is usually much to say in a very limited time for a very wide audience, one interviewer suggests that, without in any way talking down to people, it is helpful to think of compressing answers as for a twelve-year-old. Such a comment should not be taken out of context, for it reflects the interest in, and ability to receive, facts and to perceive relationships at that age, while at the same time requiring simple, clear answers.

If the interview is to run for less than five minutes it will probably stick to one major topic. But even at that a lot of information can be given, so be ready, if necessary, to limit your answers to two or three sentences per question. In the eight-to-eleven-minute format there is more chance to elaborate and give examples to clarify points; in the approximately thirty-minute interview there can be worthwhile coverage of a number of different points, and often more opportunity for an exchange of views in moments of conversation with the interviewer.

In any case, speak relatively slowly as people will take a few seconds or minutes to adjust to your delivery and personality; and, within reason, use the minimum of words to clarify your points.

Avoid whiskers such as: 'um,' 'er,' 'well,' 'you know,' 'you know what I mean,' and the like.

Think before speaking; start clearly and finish clearly. Avoid rambling.

When encouraged, and as time permits, include a personal anecdote or two. When relevant this not only illustrates a point, but helps an audience to see you as a person and not simply in a role. Few things fascinate an audience more, or are longer remembered.

In some cases there can be legal aspects involved in an interview. The simplest approach is always to make clear your position; so many people nowadays work for large organizations that it is wise to clarify whether you are speaking in an official or in a purely private capacity. In the latter case your private opinion lets the organization off the hook. No one, however, is forced to talk on the air, and you can always decline an invitation. But, if you are in any doubt about possible problems, you cannot afford to be an innocent in the matter. Consult your lawyer.

Ask whether the interview is to be edited. Because of the increasing use of taped rather than live material, many interviews are allowed to let run with the idea of half to two-thirds of the material being actually used. This is partly because some guests tend to ramble and/or be unclear and uninteresting during a proportion of the time, and because some questions will work better than others.

To a degree you have a choice about this. If you are somewhat of a VIP, you may be able to accept the invitation provided there is no editing. The alternative is to ask to hear the edited version before it goes out, or to accept the situation and trust to the editors to clarify what you have said. Many do an excellent job cutting, and so neatening away, any halting or repetition or irrelevancies.

Remember that editing the spoken word is particularly easy for radio and, though more complex for television, can, by cutting even one word, make you appear to say the opposite of what you said. Particularly dubious examples of omissions of the spoken word may come to mind from the Watergate case.

Always try to relax and be yourself. Both camera and microphone pick up artificialities quickly and, unless you are experienced, as are many actual performers or a number of politicians, tendencies towards self-doubt or hypocrisy can show.

On television wear something comfortable. Anything completely new has neither lived with you, nor you with it, and familiar clothes can help put you physically and mentally at ease.

Avoid over-gesticulation. The television screen is comparatively small and particularly suited to intimate action and response. Any action that is too much and too fast explodes around the words and may dazzle visually, but usually at the expense of content.

Once you have digested your surroundings, ignore the trappings of a television studio. Where radio is simple and intimate, involving you and a table and usually two mikes and the interviewer, (and a control room to which you nearly always have your back) a television studio can be disorienting. Clustered around the hot seats are usually two if not three cameras and, in reality, a strangely artificial set in a limbo of lights, cables, occasionally mike booms and a monitor (television screen) or two.

Leave the handling of all that side to the interviewer, for once the session has started you will be completely engrossed in what you are trying to say. Mercifully the strong lights, which have to be specially bright for colour cameras, will almost glare out your view of shadowy figures talking at near-whisper into headsets. In any case, these figures will probably look nonchalant; what is all new and bewildering about their equipment and the occasion to you, being totally everyday to them. But, in spite of apparent relaxation, their work requires a high degree of accuracy, timing, and responsibility.

You may notice cameras doing a slow spin and waltz in the gloom, and a red light appearing on one or other of them. This gives performers the knowledge of which camera to play to. But in your case always leave this to the interviewer. Unless specially requested, speak to the interviewer and not to a camera. The director up in the control room has the responsibility of getting the most interesting and valuable angles on you; these can include your response while listening as much as your expression while talking. So, although the interviewer will be shown at times, always assume that you are on camera throughout.

If, by any chance, your interviewer becomes aggressive or rude, intentionally or otherwise, ignore it. By not getting caught up in doing the same, you can leave him or her out on a limb, strengthen your position, and without fuss or wasted energy show the discerning what is happening.

But the good interviewer will avoid obvious pitfalls, and in particular will have a happy knack of recognizing that gleam in your eye when you have been asked the right question.

The interviewer

The primary function of the interviewer is to act as surrogate and ideal audience, and to be a good listener who can initiate and maintain conversation without dominating it. The role also requires the considerable inner discipline of being able to keep, not only yourself, but another and often inexperienced person on the required track. You also need an inherent sense of timing for the points at which questions can be interpolated. In addition, helped by signals from the control room or the studio director, the interviewer has to wrap up a programme within the desired x minutes or seconds before a break or the end of the show.

The above skills should also include an intuitive ability to relate to the guest, and to know when and how to be gentle or tough while remaining in control of the self and the situation, and without getting over-involved. The rare people who consistently cross these tightropes professionally often come from worlds where communication is second nature, and have a background in journalism, show business, public relations, advertising and, occasionally, teaching.

There is little direct training for interviewing, as it is one of those practical skills that can only be learned by doing. Once again some careful preparation is involved, and this will help not only in meeting someone who is usually a stranger, but also in building an adaptive confidence that can oil the cogs of the interview.

All the preparation in the world, however, will only be of value if it is designed to ask the right questions, as hinges to open the door into the other person's mind and heart. Where possible, preparation can require the use of a good reference library so as to get an all-round background about the person involved, and/or the situation he or she is being invited to talk about. One interviewer finds it takes approximately three hours to prepare for a ten-minute interview, and warns that it is important to try and become aware of any repeated mistakes carried in news items about the persons involved, varying from the date of birth to the taking-up of a special appointment, or when they arrived in a country. If, as in countless interviews, the person is not a known VIP, it is still necessary to take careful thought. Think about what the audience will want to know, and about how to handle any difficult or controversial areas tactfully yet productively. It is necessary to have an inherent sense of timing and understanding to know when a comment is complete and at which point the next question can be asked. As far as possible, especially near the beginning, or unless for special impact, avoid questions that can be answered by 'yes' or 'no.'

Included in the preparation you may need a simple background introduction to your guest. Work it over carefully so that it will evoke something of the person for the audience, and then make sure it is simple and speakable. Similarly, have a few wrap-up ideas in reserve.

Be not only a good listener but a good joiner, linking the answer to the previous question to what is to come next.

During the warm-up, or initial discussion before going on the air, which will also provide technicians with voice levels and final ideas about camera angles, avoid talk of what will actually be discussed. Your guest, and you, can easily lose track of whether a point has actually been made for the audience, taking from the main concentration and possibly not making the interview as clear as it would be otherwise.

Be interested at all times, and give the guest every benefit of your apparent total concentration. The fact that you are receiving signals about time, or about sudden mike or camera problems, should not be part of the guest's concern. And, unless you make it quite open, neither should the audience notice any distraction.

The bad interviewer:

- Doesn't know the topic, and may give the impression of barely knowing who the guest is
- Never gets to a question
- Talks too much
- Opinionates
- Makes no relationship between answers and coming questions
- Asks very involved questions
- Asks multiple questions.

The good interviewer:

- Asks for interesting answers
- Does not talk too much, and is not opinionated
- May have various styles, but can call on a quality of brevity
- Can put the crunch question without giving offence and, if not satisfied, press for more of an answer
- Lets the questions do the work and keeps own personality in the background.

An important part of the interviewer's function is to relax the guest and to help him or her feel at ease and at home as soon as possible.

Avoid any tendency to repeat answers. This takes time, makes what has been said redundant, and is an indication of your lack of preparedness for the next question.

The one time, however, when some repetition can be helpful is when your guest comes from another country and is not too proficient at speaking your language. If the guest's accent and expression might be a barrier to comprehension by the average listener, then quick clarification may help.

Because it is necessary for you to be an easy person for your guest to meet, it is important to realize that you will need to use the outgoingness of your personality. Within this factor there are certain performance techniques, which may help elucidate the interesting answer. These include trying to get politicians, for example, to comment or to elaborate on points on which they may be somewhat unwilling to speak.

Then there is the antagonist approach, which attempts, by often prefacing the question with a large or small barb, to make the guest give a more illuminating answer than otherwise. Similarly, there is the silence technique, which may be used after the guest feels an answer is complete. It is only human that he should want to fill the rather surprising gap. Responsibly and tactfully used, this technique may well bring out yet reluctant thoughts and feelings. Another way of drawing a person out is literally to peter out in raising a point or starting a question – and thus letting the guest do the filling in.

Such techniques, however, can rebound as, should the guest be experienced in their use and wish to be difficult, he can extend them back to the interviewer, and the effect can lead to personal duelling rather than the elucidation of a situation.

Interviewers who are experienced in both radio and television find that radio is a less formal and more frank medium, because it is more anonymous. For the same reason, guests are usually less nervous and lose any self-consciousness earlier. In radio, interest relies solely on what is said and how it is said, and there can be no complementary visual signals.

Finally, all interviews hinge upon that vital rapport between interviewer and guest which is still, as the head announcer of a large broadcasting corporation said recently, 'largely a matter of chemistry.'

Voice routine

Continue as before. Include relaxation, keep the breathing deep and wide, and always check ease of movement and posture. Look in a mirror occasionally to see that the shoulders remain level. Our perception of balance is related to the way we usually hold ourselves; habit feels comfortable and right. If someone who carries the right shoulder a bit high is asked to relax and lower it, he or she may comment that it then feels crooked, and for a while may need to check the look rather than the feel.

Increase the scope of practice on vowel sounds from the main, long sounds to include the short sounds, included below, the long sounds being underlined:

Lip vowels   *Tongue vowels*
Thr_ou_gh g_oo_d t_o_ne _a_ll n_o_t   p_ar_t m_u_st s_er_ve _a_nd then sh_a_pe f_i_t sp_ee_ch

While the tongue helps shape all vowels, being raised at the back and gradually lowered during the first five vowels above, the lips are essential in moulding their shape. Then, with the jaw continuing to remain open throughout, the tongue takes over, rising towards the front of the mouth as the tip stays, as always for vowels, lightly resting and out of the way on the lower front teeth.

When you have practised that sentence a few times, make your own list of words containing these sounds; and try to find another sentence to contain them. This will help you know that your ear has caught the intended sounds and can recognize their use.

Note where you find the long and short vowels in the following passage, which needs full ease and quiet resonance of voice. Before starting, think of saturating yourself with the awful calm; and see if you can catch a sense of the strangeness of the motion followed by a particular kind of stillness.

Till noon we quietly sailed on,
Yet never a breeze did breathe.
Slowly and smoothly went the ship,
Moved onward from beneath.

Under the keel nine fathoms deep,
From the land of mist and snow,
The spirit slid; and it was he
That made the ship to go.
The sails at noon left off their tune,
And the ship stood still also.

From *The Rime of the Ancient Mariner*, Coleridge

When you feel you are making progress with your voice work, this is a challenging poem to speak in its entirety. The impact and growing terror of the legend will take all your concentration; but the words lie under the tongue, if sometimes quaintly, as notes in music. Try to encompass the experience as if you were speaking it to, and sharing it with, someone else. If you like, make a rough tape of a section. But do not initially expect all to ring true; some verses will take off better than others. You can return, re-envision, and polish such work, as it becomes known in your bones, over a period of some years.

Since the words of many songs are essentially speakable and musical and have a strong rhythm, they are an excellent source of patter exercises. For lightness, agility, and practice of that quick, silent intake of breath, look at folk songs, and at two songs popularized by Burl Ives, 'The Owl and the Pussy-cat' by Edward Lear, and the traditional 'There was an Old Woman who Swallowed a Fly.' Always remember that such exercises are not ends in themselves. They are simply a means of limbering mind, heart, and voice so that they are in tune for that gradual transition into ease and flexibility during everyday, and possibly public, use.

Assignments

– Starting with a five- or ten-minute format, interview a friend or member of your class or group on a topic that is familiar to them, but less so to a general public and to you.

– Similarly, arrange to be interviewed yourself.
– Once the topics are chosen, each interviewer has time to consider what the public would want to know, and so the kind of questions to have ready.

Listen to professional interviewers on radio and television, not to become a carbon copy, but to be more aware of the craft of question and response. Note whether a guest evades, goes off point, or opens to a situation.

Over a period of some months, try to make time to interview friends, acquaintances, and contacts, using your tape recorder if all concerned are willing. There is no substitute for widening your range by doing.

Meanwhile avoid any assumption that initial assignments are too simple to present too much of a challenge. They can help development according to the care and preparation you give them; taken superficially, they could produce superficial results. Remember that it is better to start with a simple positive experience to build into memory than to rush into something ambitious too early – for example, an interview that may take up thirty minutes of air time, and which should stand the test of public interest.

As you listen to a playback of your interview, check for:

– Clarity of questions, including what is asked and how it is asked
– Appropriate length of answer within the overall time available
– Any overlap between voices or sense of interruption
– Hesitations or verbal whiskers on either side.

Finally, put yourself in the place of a listener who knows neither of you. Would the interview attract attention, hold interest, and be informative? Would a listener remember it, and possibly want to tell someone else about it later?

10
Using The Phone, Job Interviews

If a world-wide vote could be taken on the question, 'What, after the wheel, has been the most useful invention in everyday life?' it is more than likely that the answer would be 'the telephone.' So much do we take it for granted that, like the personal resource of imagination mentioned in Chapter 1, it is possible to appreciate it most if we consider life without it.

There would be no easy access to anybody; a reliance on letters with speed of delivery varying according to distance; no fast answers; no chance to talk out a problem before making an informed decision. Most of our business and much of our social life would come to a standstill. Imagine that all the networks connected with telephone lines, such as major computer operations, telex, cable television, telegrams and undersea cable, have been cut. Our world would seem to revert back into an antediluvian era of the mail coach, pony express, semaphore, and smoke signal.

It is interesting to realize that the final form of this wonderful invention came from the inquiring mind of a man versed in the human needs of speaking and listening. Young Alexander Graham Bell was not only to become a great inventor, but from his father had inherited the gifts and knowledge that enabled him to establish an international reputation as a teacher of the deaf. In this role he supplies us with an example of a point raised in the chapter on interviewing. Thinking deeply about the possibility of sending not just one, but multiple impulses along a telegraph wire, he began to ask the right question. Instead of developing means of sending mechanical codes in vibrating sequence, why not send the actual vibrations of the human voice with its own code of speech?

Now his invention is at the root of our spoken communications, and of our immediate ability to send and receive information beyond previous barriers of time and space. We range from a president speaking to a man on the moon, to the teenager whose existence depends on nightly conversation with close friends.

But within our world-wide systems there are varied attitudes to use of the phone, some depending on economics, and some on cultural differences. It comes as a surprise to the North American that in England, for example, the phone is a part of the postal service, and that because of sheer pressure of use, in addition to rent and long-distance rates, charges are made for each call. But the cut-off time from public booths is even more surprising, and this coupled with the comparative costs of long-distance calls makes for an approach that does not allow time to waste words. In North America where there is as yet no individual charge, habits are more relaxed. The phone can still be an instrument for passing time, and with rising costs of travel it is likely to remain the prime means of conquering distance. Another interesting difference in attitude, and so use, is that on the west side of the Atlantic a gadget seems to take precedence over human presence, and there is a tendency to allow the phone to interrupt a conversation. With the result that when it is made clear no calls will be accepted for a while, the accolade of complete attention is about to be given.

And whereas a great poet noted over three hundred years ago that 'No man is an island,' we might today add the echo, 'And man is everywhere accessible.' For the phone, particularly where used in conjunction with a paging, or bleep-system, can invade our lives at any time or in any place. To some it has become such a mixed blessing that they retreat behind an unlisted number; while to others one of the blessings of a good holiday can be that the phone never rings for them.

General use of the phone

Because the phone puts us in touch with the sound rather than the sight of another person, it is self-evident that it reflects everything through the voice. As mentioned in Chapter 5, under vocal signals, we can be intuitively aware of how a friend feels as soon as they answer, though naturally we try to avoid letting through personal ups and downs when speaking to acquaintances or business contacts.

Keep a note-pad and pencil handy by every phone you use. Some people have marvellous memories for messages, including other numbers and addresses. Most of us need a jog from the written word.

Always identify yourself clearly, particularly in business when people will want to hear your name and possibly your function. And it is helpful to remember in the home, for example, how you can be mistaken for another member of the family; just as you may cheerfully say 'Hullo, Sheila,' when it's her sister, Jill, or 'Hi! Tom,' when it's his brother Jack. This is because the phone uses an inexpensive form of microphone and speaker to reproduce the matter, rather than the whole manner, including the usual overtones and resonance, of your speech. But naturally the message is also conveyed by intonation, which, as we discussed in Chapter 4, may also be used in a similar pattern by other members, usually of your generation, of your tribe. And speech, as we know, is still very much an imitative tribal affair.

When using the phone, be yourself, or – for business or professional purposes – an extension of yourself. Gone are the days of long ago, when because maintaining volume was a technical problem, the phone was regarded as some foreign devil that had to be cranked up and shouted into. There are, however, still a few people who feel shy and sound reluctant to use the phone, and the occasional tyrant among minor officials, or among secretaries, who seem happy to set up a barrier between public and boss. While this can be done with courtesy and consideration, if it is not, the public may wonder if this is intentional or if the boss doesn't know and, if not, why not?

There is one group of people that, with travel becoming universal, can sometimes make the phone difficult for all of us. A foreigner with limited knowledge of our language can have a problem in using the new vocabulary and syntax and, at the same time, listening to them without the complementary language of facial expression and gesture. When receiving such a call, be patient; indicate interest and comprehension as clearly as you can; encourage where possible and be prepared to take extra time.

MAKING A CALL

When using the phone, as with all effective communication, be clear in your own mind about what you want to say and how you want to say it. Experience helps, but it can be a good idea to rehearse things so you can best express them within the context of the situation. This will avoid an impression of uncertainty and the confusion that often comes from backtracking; and it will save time. It will also sound as if you are capable of that important element in a transaction, of speaking in terms that makes immediate sense to the other person.

One of the frustrating elements about use of the phone comes when you summon ideas and energy, and Mr X is not there. His number may be engaged, he may be temporarily out of the office, out of town, or out of the country or at a meeting. If you feel the matter will be best discussed when you have your facts, figures, and concentration ready, it may be best to keep initiating the call rather than leave a message. Unless you have a secretary, his return call may catch you off-balance when you are immersed in other things.

Unfortunately, the more gadgets we possess, the more the human element seems to get lost, so it can be useful to develop the habit of asking, informally, the name of the person taking the message. This provides a means of your contact being able to trace any repeated or serious lapses in the message-taking process.

When initiating a business call, aim to sound alive and competent. No one is going to put much faith in a request for an interview or idea for a meeting if it sounds dull, incoherent, or disinterested. It would, in fact, be interesting to take a tally of the amount of business subconsciously lost and gained by the dismal tone of some voices and the lively tone of others. So much is talked, written about, and financed concerning the public relations aspect of almost any kind of organization, that it might also be valuable for everyone from executive to receptionist to appreciate that relating to the public begins right with the voice on the phone.

Use short, simple sentences. Avoid rambling and make explanations clear. Don't dawdle as if the other person had all day. Before giving an order or specific directions, have all your facts ready, including any necessary numbers, times, dates, addresses, or spelling. Do as you would be done by, and avoid ripping through an order or barking a message. Always avoid two people trying to give the same facts at the same time. Do away with grunts, mumbles, and whispers, and remember that the phone is an open line to a useful relationship between speaker and listener.

ANSWERING A CALL

In many cases your answer may be the first contact people make with your organization, so however pressured or bored you may be, sound alert and interested. If you are a woman, it may be taken for granted that you are a secretary, so to avoid misunderstandings it may be helpful to indicate the level of your work.

In areas where there is considerable contact with the public, keep the voice level and stay even-tempered. If callers are rude or aggressive, do not answer in kind; ignore their tone or language, and keep to the point of the business at hand. If someone becomes abusive, let a supervisor or boss know; if it is really bad, disconnect.

Keep message forms and pencil handy. And in most organizations it is useful to have lists of information that is often required. These can be especially useful to an understudy when the secretary is out to lunch. They may include other phone numbers and addresses and, above all, who is in, who out, and when they may be expected to return.

Be able to convey information without it sounding like a formula. What is dull and routine to you is new and will have significance for the caller. Similarly, if connected to a paging system, avoid a droning automaton sound. Nothing is more dreary for either patients or visitors in hospital, for example, than to hear the most depressing sounding calls for doctors or special staff. In fact anyone who is in touch with the public through any system would do well to borrow a tape-recorder occasionally – not to plug into the others involved, but simply to listen to their own voice for personal evaluation.

Aim to listen carefully to the caller's name. Make a point of jotting it down, or memorizing and using it before the end of the conversation. It adds a considerate touch, and the caller knows you are alert, and will appreciate a sense of recognitiion that can be extended during any office call at a later date.

When a message comes, note it down right away and put it in the appropriate slot or on the desk immediately. If necessary, have a system ready so that if things are specially busy, all slips are visible and await everyone's return. No one knows the full significance of a call to another person. When there is time it is also useful to repeat the message. Accurate listening is an important factor in saving time, avoiding misunderstandings, and building confidence among colleagues and associates. It should be balanced by the equal need to relay any message within the spirit of the sender's intent.

Job interviews

Everyone faces interviews of various kinds and levels in their lives, ranging from completing a form and then seeing a personnel representative of, say, a large store, to one-day safaris before a selection board leading to its final decision from a coveted short list.

Job interviews can be time-consuming, mundane, and, as in much human transaction, occasionally annoying and sometimes fascinating. But in the long run they can be rewarding and a decided learning experience. Each will be different, but each time you can build on factors arising from being wise after the event, such as avoiding rushed answers, or knowing some of the questions that are likely to be put. Occasionally the answer to the simplest, most obvious question is the hardest, as when the prospective student applying for training is asked, 'Why do you want to paint – or act – or teach?'

Similarly, in all fields there are stock, but potentially loaded, questions such as 'What gifts – or experience – or training do you have which would be of particular value in this position?'

Most interviews include some minutes of conversation designed to put you at your ease. These also enable the representatives of the organization to assess your ability to meet, interact, and express yourself among comparative strangers. For it is important to bear in mind that, particularly in interviews affecting promotion, the ability to use the spoken word with ease in terms of both what you say and how you say it can be a key factor. In the growing complexities and interdependence of corporate, business, and professional life, merely knowing the job is not enough. Communication of both expectations and results is equally important, and the candidate with a keep-it-to-himself mumble or an inability to explain a process, or to answer simple questions simply, can lose out over one apparently less qualified or experienced. As a placement officer of an international organization noted recently, 'It is essential that candidates speak effectively if fair assessment is to be made of their potential.'

BEFORE THE INTERVIEW
Public relations, as mentioned in the last section, should be regarded as just as important for an individual as for a large corporation. Aim to make a good presentation of yourself, whether from the viewpoint of an initial phone call, an advance letter, or general grooming. Have facts on your background down on paper, and also fresh in mind. Then you do not have to sound vague or fumble about dates or about why you left previous jobs. Remember that references are likely to be required, and it is a good idea to mention this need to responsible friends or colleagues in advance.

It can be helpful to find out something about the organization in advance, the type of people they are looking for, and particular jobs that may be open. Some interviews are for immediate needs; some are part of a continuing process in which your details may be filed for future reference.

Allow extra time for the journey, and aim to arrive with a few minutes to spare. Better to collect thoughts for a while, take in the atmosphere, and listen to what else is going on, than arrive breathless and feeling rushed. Use the opportunity to go over your own list of questions which, with a reasonable firm, you may be expected to ask. These cover not only salary and future openings, but fringe benefits, actual location, and job description.

During the interview
Be honest. Do not try to pull the wool over the interviewers' eyes. They are experienced at sizing people up and selecting suitable applicants. Interviews

take time and are therefore an invisible cost; and the lower the turnover of employees, the better. And while there is usually an understanding of the way in which a degree of nerves can affect people, try to avoid the extremes of saying too much – or too little.

Listen carefully to questions and, without being over-hesitant, take your time with your answers. Be prepared to say why you left previous jobs without being over-elaborate, and to give a summary of your range of experience. Avoid curtness or, unless indicated, mere 'yes' or 'no' answers. Aim to make your information as simple and clear as possible, assessing by any visual or verbal feedback whether you are giving what is required.

Remember that this use of the spoken word, while not uttered for public consumption, in terms of audience, still requires some extension or outerance of yourself. Being interviewed is not just a passive affair, and results will largely depend on your own quiet management of the situation.

Do not be concerned if at some point the interview appears to take off on an apparently unconnected topic. An indication of your ability to improvise may be helpful; and there may be a need to relax for a few minutes.

Be observant about signals indicating the near, and actual, end of the interview. Applicants who have to be walked out of an office while still talking may demonstrate an unfortunate blind spot. When you are told that that is all and are thanked for coming, reply in kind and, if it has been a worthwhile experience, extend your thanks for the time given. Move out of the room easily; remember that last impressions can be just as important as first.

Voice routine

Continue work on your initial preparation and relaxation exercises.
Maintain practice of breathing and humming.
Review the previous addition of vowel sounds, and your list of words containing them.

Here are four more sounds, this time known as diphthongs, being an amalgamation of two now familiar sounds. They are often thought of as glides within a syllable, and it is helpful to think of them initially as moving in slow motion from the starting towards the finishing sound.

- Go from the vowel in luck towards the vowel in lit and you get the vowel in line.
- Go from the long 'a' in last towards the vowel in look and you get the vowel in loud.
- Go from the vowel in lot towards the vowel in lit and you get the first vowel in loiter.

– Go from the vowel in l*i*t towards the vowel in l*oo*k and you get that in l*u*te.

Such blends can give you an insight into some of the interesting variations of the accents of English. For example, the last sound, as in l*u*te, is not used in some North American regions. In this case what others regard as the customary start of the glide disappears, and the monophthong, or single sound, as in sh*oe* is substituted. This could result in hearing that the 'Dook of Edinborough has gone to buy a noospaper.' In some regions of England, Ireland, and Newfoundland, the sound as in l*i*ne tends to begin with the sound as in l*o*t rather than as that in l*u*ck. This could result in hearing about the 't*oi*me' of day rather than the t*i*me of day.

The diphthong as in l*ou*d is often a signal of hurt, or of pain, as in 'Ow!' or even 'Ouch!'. The mental equivalent, which can also be a springboard for expression of happiness, is usually signified by 'Oh.' Consider how sound colours expression when, in Shaw's *Pygmalion* or the musical version, *My Fair Lady*, Eliza, not yet quite the lady, is surprised by a vision of her father, the dustman. He is resplendent in morning suit and on the way to his wedding. Shaw gives her an elasticated gasp that glides round every aspect of her astonishment with his writing of 'A-a-a-a-a-ah-ow-ooh.' What a world of contrast to the then socially acceptable, 'Oh.'

Assignments

Here it can be helpful to simulate the job interview situation for a number of reasons: 1 / because of specific needs, it can give confidence in the use of your own words within a situation upon which much in your life may depend; 2 / it can provide a dry run for an actuality which occurs at different levels many times in our lives; and 3 / by switching your role from applicant to interviewer and vice versa, it can give you a valuable understanding of both sides of a situation.

You can find many helpful comments on job interviews in books on business education. But remember that in our print-oriented society we sometimes forget to use that most valuable source of material – the oral tradition – known as the horse's mouth. So extend the work of the previous chapter and see if you, or a member of your class or group with contacts, could arrange to interview an interviewer. Avoid thinking in terms of everyone fanning out to similar organizations because they could return with an amount of repetitive material, and it is best to regard any such giving of time as a privilege extended out of special interest, rather than as a right that can be expected every so often. Ask the official concerned if you could bring a tape-recorder, and then see how much useful information he or she would share with you over, say, a twenty-minute period. Remember that, in addition to the routine needs of his or her organization, each interviewer is likely to have some personal comment on what he or she looks for in assessing an applicant.

– Prepare a ten-minute oral report for your group.
– Avoid the temptation to have the group just sit and listen to your tape of the interview (see ideas on assessment at the end of Chapter 15).
– Use the occasion for further practice in the valuable exercise of selecting and synthesizing material for others, and within a given time.
– Divide off and, on the basis of any previous experience and such research, take some dry runs at interviews of many kinds and at different levels, as noted in this chapter.

11

Making and Receiving Complaints, and the Art of Demonstrating

The need to be effective in making and receiving complaints can become a necessary element of survival in our increasingly bureaucratic and techno-logical society. While we generally live among marvels and benefits, when something goes wrong on the production line or along the administrative chain, it may seem difficult to stop the momentum and seek correction of errors or mistakes. Unfortunately, the more nuts and bolts we live among, the more can be wrongly assembled; and sometimes the longer the chain of messages and memos between people, the harder it seems to communicate. It can be invisibly easy, particularly when under pressure, for example, to transpose a word or numeral, or slightly change the intent of a message whether as given or received.

The obtaining of a correction or rectifying of a situation is usually effected by use of the spoken word, either on the phone or by personal meeting. Gone are the days when many people would take time to sit down and write the matter out; or even dictate a letter and have a secretary type it, with copies, containing all facts and figures. Again, as in the chapter on interview-ing for radio and television, we have a situation which lends itself to interest-ing assignments, and to development of confidence in the use of the spoken word. Dry runs, or rehearsals, of the situation from the viewpoint of both making and receiving complaints, can help us understand both sides of a potentially difficult element in human communication.

To begin at the beginning: no one likes to be corrected, especially for a mistake they have not made. Which brings us to the heart of one of the major barriers to getting a quick and satisfactory response to a bona fide complaint. For, during the conduct of today's world there is often a chasm, sometimes created by administration, between the complainant and the per-son responsible.

The problem may be the mere nuisance of having to return goods obviously damaged in transit, or occasional canned or frozen food in bad condition. It may include having to deal with a serious error in billing, with an unacceptable standard of repair, with a matter of opinion concerning a radio or television programme, or with poor value and strange practice as in double-booking by a travel agent.

Making complaints

Realize that a complaint often has to be traced to its source, and on the way be put before a number of people before it can be rectified. So, although a nuisance, it can be advisable to keep sales slips and receipts. Then, if a new raincoat changes colour and shrinks the first time it is cleaned, or a heel comes off a pair of shoes within a month of purchase, the details are at hand.

Remember that the person you first approach is unlikely to be responsible for, or to know about, the causes of your complaint, or even to have any connection with the matter; so avoid coming on strong and making demands for redress without giving any explanation. It is better to think in terms of enlisting help, which you are going to need, than engaging antagonism. It can be imagined how the initial person, and others down the line, would respond if the approach were curt, unfriendly and, as some report, even brutal. Meanwhile, if you are hot-tempered, wait for your feelings to cool. An emotional tirade may let off steam, but may lead only to confrontation and conflict.

Bear in mind that the person on the other end of the phone, or behind the desk, is a human being too, and gather your energy for repetition of the matter and a probable time-lag between voicing your need and gaining a result. Assume this will be positive, but be prepared to be persistent, as in the case of the student who, in requesting a copy of his academic record for entry into professional training school, found he could make no application because his record had been lost. He saw everyone from registrar to dean, to thirty-five officials and, finally, the minister concerned. His most appalled comment was that no one, not even the minister, would take responsibility. However, someone finally gave the go-ahead on the basis of 'don't tell anyone I told you,' and the next day the lost papers reappeared in the mail.

Have your records in front of you, but put the onus on the other party to corroborate facts in your favour. Instead of telling them you paid your bill, ask them to look in their files with their record of the transaction, and you may more quickly gain their co-operation. Similarly, if they agree there is no balance owing, yet by some chance you are still pestered, they are the more likely to take fast and more remedial action. Ask for the name or some identification of the person you are talking to. Should you get no satisfaction the first time, you have a starting point of reference if you ever need to take matters to the top of the organization.

Be understanding of the representative, but honest and persistent about what you want. Keep your voice level and reasonable; there may eventually be some form of compromise, but show by what you say and how you say it that you will not be put off or sidetracked.

It is worth remembering that the days are gone when products and service were uncomplicated, competition for individual custom keen, and the customer always right. A percentage of complainants are out to make false claims, and in some cases an organization has to safeguard their interests and double-check certain complaints.

Receiving complaints

Somewhere along the line most of us receive complaints, if not about our particular jobs, then in connection with the organization we work for; and some people spend a large part of their working lives in handling such problems.

Though experience is the greatest mainstay, some general points can help, of which the most obvious is: be a good listener. This factor can not only pour oil on often troubled waters, but is essential to the outcome of the situation. Facts that you pass on must be clear and accurate, or will lead only to further complication when related down the line. And because you may have heard only one side of the question, you have to use special tact, for you don't fully know what happened.

Be reasonable and sound reasonable. If somebody uses a style of attack in their voice, de-fuse the situation; explain you are not directly responsible and can help best by first getting the facts. If, as occasionally happens, a person is emotionally wrought and beyond sensible reality, try to see the situation with them and then get them to the point of being cheerful about something. When they are rational, explain what you need to know and what you will try to do. Unfortunately, a bad previous experience can make a person suspicious of your attempts from the start; it is human to dread any repeat of a negative experience. Guided by your observation and intuition, you may find it useful to use humour, without disrespect to the person or situation, to let in a sense of proportion and show some basis of mutual understanding.

You may, however, need to be perceptive as to whether someone is trying to deceive you by giving a biased version of events. In which case, a brashness or even bombast may lead to a loud voice, sweeping gestures and a veritable sense of cover-up of real facts and issues. Another form of insecurity can lead to a sense of suspicion and clamming-up concerning the facts you need to know.

There are people who consider that every untoward situation that evolves round them is an emergency, and who demand action to be taken this minute; in which case, be prepared to make immediate assessment. For example, can a piece of plumbing wait if a pipe leaks after regular hours, or must someone be called in when overtime rates would be in effect?

Avoid sounding impersonal. Be considerate of the fact that, while the situation probably has no personal involvement for you, it can be a matter of some import for the person concerned. Likewise steer clear of any sense of boredom or ridicule. Negative antagonism can be quickly felt, can make some people more vulnerable, and will be unlikely to give a person much confidence in your co-operation. Aim to reduce bad feeling, and to show willing and take appropriate action, for a positive outcome can be a strong element in public, and future, relations.

A credibility gap

While these comments may be applicable where there is integrity on both sides of a complaint, remember that, just as there are customers who make false claims, there are also organizations who put up a false front about backing their products and correcting mistakes. Should you as consumer realize from growing evidence and false promise that you have been given a bad deal and the firm has little intention of making adequate repair or refund, it may be helpful to use other strategies. A lady whose washing machine neither worked nor was serviced properly after months of requests put it on her front lawn, framed by flags and streamers and topped with a large notice of all its problems, and sent a colour photograph to the firm's executives. The offending appliance was collected and a new one installed next day.

If contact with the higher echelons of an organization yields nothing, it may be necessary to take your problems into the public domain and air the facts, which must be accurate, on a radio or television show, or in an article. Granted all this is a bothersome activity, and further strategies are outside the content of this book, but producers and public can take notice when they realize the implications of buying and selling a particular product or dealing with a certain organization.

In these days of the sheer bigness of everything, we may seem to have little choice in this selection of alternatives, and sometimes in expecting responsible answers to community doubts about government and corporate action. The wheel is turning, however, and people are beginning to talk back to officials and air their views and their voices through a positive use of words that is often heartfelt and leaves no doubt about the clarity of their intent.

But, as noted by the rental agent of a large apartment complex, whose job is concerned with every kind of person, and who keeps a steely integrity inside a charmingly velvet glove, 'Complaints require courtesy and consideration on either side, and it doesn't hurt to give a little of both.'

The art of demonstrating

It is fitting to include in our section on the use of your own words some comment on the use of the spoken word during the demonstration of a new skill, or a process or, occasionally, a discovery. For while demonstration is a largely visual activity, the spoken word in this case is usually more satisfactory than the written word. Think, for example, of assembling a do-it-yourself product from written instructions and diagrams, compared to actually hearing the voice of the instructor, and often seeing the end result before trying for oneself.

Furthermore, like other topics we have covered, demonstration can give excellent practice in effective communication. It usually provides the immediate feedback of question or of discussion, or of achievement by doing. So either the observers can understand and possibly repeat the skill, or they can't. And if not, provided they are genuinely using that essential resource of E for effort, the responsibility rests with the instructor to clarify and recheck needs within the context of the situation.

Good demonstration is an art which forms the basis of a considerable amount of teaching, and so is the means by which we learn a large proportion of important skills at every age and level of our lives. The need can arise in the home, at the office, in school, in many forms of selling, or just plain on the job, as in explaining a procedure to a newcomer. It can extend from helping a child tie a shoe-lace, to giving a lecture-demonstration in the arts, to showing new and sophisticated techniques in the sciences. It is a key factor in much construction, from building with blocks to working with heavy equipment; in success in sports, from the swing of a racquet to the spin of a ball; and often in safety, from the handling of chemicals to the control of a car in a skid.

Whatever the purpose of a demonstration, the principle is the same: to clarify a process for one, or one hundred or some thousands or more people, in a way which they can understand and if necessary repeat and develop, with appropriate confidence, for themselves.

The requirements for a good demonstration include the following:

- Know what you are doing. If you are uncertain of the procedure in any way, you are likely not only to sound it, because much of your message will come through your voice, but to look it, since unease is quickly transmitted to fingers and thumbs and posture. Even worse, the observers could become fumblefingers.
- Prepare a demonstration as carefully as a speech. This applies as much to the software of ideas as to care in the assembly of any hardware. All equipment should be in good condition and, like any notes, arranged and ready in order of use.
- Think about the demonstration with special consideration for the needs and experience of the observers. Put yourself imaginatively for a while in their place and ask, 'If this material was new to me, how could it be presented so that it would be as clear and interesting as possible?'
- Plan your demonstration as the production, or showing, of an event. Realize that it may need as much time for rehearsal of the motions as for delivery of the knowledge and ideas within your notes. Aim to let the words, and the way they are spoken, complement the visual element; and remember to leave time for any questions and comments.
- Brief introduction, which, to ensure interest, may be hooked by anecdote or by case history to a relevant context. Sometimes started by some humour, this can sharpen attention and can help any wayward minds appreciate the value of the work involved.
- Statement of background knowledge and theory, which may in some cases be a necessary form of review of previous material.
- Let the action then take over, so that the spoken word acts as a quiet commentary on the skills involved. Avoid any blurring of such lines, for an instructor who creates an overlap and tries to do two, if not three, things at once will rarely convey a memorable image, or impart competence in the activity.

Be sure that the action is smooth and controlled, letting every picture or motion tell a story that can be remembered. You may well find here that an interesting phenomenon occurs that can hardly be measured, but is more likely sensed. For while you are showing the process, a part of your mind's eye will be viewing it from the observer's viewpoint; similarly, many observers will be making infinitesimal movements as if to help both memory and understanding. The clearer these reciprocating movements, the more easily observers will be able to learn the activity.

Where this degree of visual participation is well exercised, and where there is economy in the movement, a demonstration can become particularly memorable, even if it is for the purpose of making a point rather than stimulating a specific activity. For example, a great French mime, or exponent of the art of silent acting, Etienne Decroux, who was the teacher of a gifted performer of the next generation, Marcel Marceau, once demonstrated the everyday muddle of movement involved in a man climbing into a raincoat. Then he showed the liquidity of the same action achieved with a flowing co-ordination. The difference was as chalk from cheese, and has remained in the memory for over twenty years.

He also used a method which is particularly effective in gaining maximum effect with great simplicity by using the do/don't approach, which is often used in advertising within the before/after syndrome.

- Divide the total process into steps of achievement. A large part of the essence of any such instruction lies in being prepared to break down knowledge into components. For example, a little of this, and a little of that, satisfactorily achieved, is initially preferable to one long run that leaves observers both out of mental breath and with a sense of visual/verbal indigestion. Within such a framework, a difficulty may be immediately caught and worked on, and small misunderstandings need not go unnoticed and create delays later.
- Allow time for questions so that any part of the demonstration can be explored in greater detail or depth, or allusion made to possible future development and application.

Thus there can be a fascination and delight in a good demonstration on the part of the instructor, in having passed on new knowledge and skills; and on the part of the observers in the interest and challenge in acquiring them. And, for our overall purpose in developing use of the skills of communication, practice in demonstration is also useful as an aid to furthering confidence. This is largely because by its very nature a demonstration requires the use of material outside the self. This gives an additional focus of attention which can help take pressure off any residue of self-consciousness. It also enables the speaker to become quickly engrossed in the presentation of the information and the activity of the learning involved.

Voice routine

Review work on the vowel sounds known as diphthongs, which were introduced in the previous voice routine at the end of Chapter 10. Diphthongs, composed of two short sounds followed by the neutral, short *er*, sound, form the basis of triphthongs. The three sounds in this category are:

the long vowels as in h*i*ger, flo*wer* and y*our*

The last of these sounds, as in y*our*, meets with few variations. The sound as in flo*wer* is sometimes distorted by a narrow and nasal start, resembling more the vowel in c*a*t than in b*a*lm. Then it is helpful to isolate the first element, making sure the tongue position is lower and closer to the long than to the short 'a.' When the sound has been re-shaped – avoiding any plumminess as in the 'how-now-brown-cow' syndrome – try it in a few words and phrases. Continue to monitor it when reading aloud, realizing that past habit may want to predominate for a while.

Assignments

MAKING AND RECEIVING COMPLAINTS

As suggested in the job interview situation, if you are in a group or class, a member could ask to interview someone whose job is connected with receiving complaints. If agreed, the interview could be taped, and the member return with a ten-minute report summarizing the gist of the interview. Later, when time is available, it would be interesting for some of the group to hear the recording so that they could compare it with the report. They might feel they would have made similar comments, or have handled their impressions differently, or have done so in the same way. In some cases those interviewed may ask for a recording of the report, and their views on this could make for an interesting further response.

The preparation of such reports is similar to the work needed before giving a speech, but will need to be as informative as possible. Try to avoid the temptation to repeat a list of answers to questions along the lines of, 'I asked this, and he or she said that; and then I asked that, and he or she said this.'

People who have something useful to tell you could include those who work in large stores, in any form of rental business, or in some government offices.

– Work out, with a partner, a variety of situations in which one of you has to make a legitimate complaint.
– For example, you buy some frozen food, but when you come to cook it you find it is in a very mushy state. How will you approach the store manager?
– Or you and your wife, husband, or friend go away for a package-style

holiday and find the accommodation below standard. How do you approach the hotel manager while you are there, or the travel agent when you return?

DEMONSTRATIONS

Ideas for demonstrations can be as extensive as the world is round. They can include the arts, the sciences, medicine, trades, sports, crafts, and hobbies. They can be as long as an hour or more, or as brief as a sales pitch in a large store. And they can fall within the same categories of purpose as other forms of speaking in public – to inform, persuade, instruct, and entertain – though they can again include elements of all. And it can be a useful practice to evoke some humour, especially initially, to give a sense of contrast and proportion to the event.

Occasionally, it does no harm to take a usually serious situation and turn it to lighter account. For example, architecture students taking a course in speech communication were once invited to demonstrate any hobby they wished; but they were expected to use less than the usual equipment. One contributed a notably earnest demonstration about skin-diving using an elderly, cylinder-type vacuum cleaner for an air tank, a pair of 1910 driving goggles for a mask, and other assorted properties straight out of the attic.

Tipping a situation over into the surprise of the unexpected is at the root of much humour, so try some assignments along lighter lines. They will give experience in the special timing of listener-response, and this cannot be learned by being talked about. It has to be done; in fact, self-demonstrated. You will find more comments on comedy in Chapter 15, 'Reading aloud,' under the heading, 'The dramatic form.'

12
Words Social

An essential factor of our ability to function in life lies in our need to relate to other people. This is largely achieved through turning the impulse of thought and feeling into the spoken word. Understandably, as in Chapter 5, this is still an edited word, being filtered not only through the resources of personality and knowledge, but through our ability to match expression to impulse. It is also edited through consideration of others involved, though the more relaxed the relationship the less we are conscious of taking extra care. And when there is a happy meeting of underlying values and interests, we often talk of such contact in terms of 'speaking the same language.'

An interesting concept about the way we use our voices, particularly in a social context, is that during the course of civilization the sound of voicing has taken over from the sense of touching. We now tend to make contact more through the significance of sound than through the sensation of touch, with speaking becoming a form of vocal stroking. So we get murmurs and purrs of reassurance from dentists and doctors, of encouragement from teachers, and of affection from relatives and friends. Conversely, when we wish to suggest we are out of tune with another person or group, it may come to mind that we use the voice to sound impersonal, uncaring, and out of touch, or distant.

One aspect of the need to use our own words which causes concern to some people is that sense of being put on the spot and realizing that talking, especially to strangers, often requires conscious effort. It is as if we have to extend resources that, in a familiar situation as with family and friends, we use with unconscious ease. So it comes about that there may be a gap, hopefully only momentary, after saying 'hullo,' or between topics of conversation. But the real worry, which can become akin to some of the problems discussed in the section on nerves before speaking in public, lies in what to do if that gap lengthens. It can land us back in that tongue-tied situation of being literally at a loss for words; but in this case, not with some time for preparation, or even gaining a solo run at a topic, but in having to participate with someone, or many other people, in a totally improvised form of dialogue of which nobody knows the outcome.

Participation upon such open ice has perhaps two prerequisites. One, as mentioned in Chapter 6, concerns the fundamental trust and sense of confidence we have in our own selves, which we can then extend to others. It is easy to forget, for example, that when men shake hands they are not using a mere form of greeting, but a symbolic gesture stemming from a centuries-old need, indicating that by a clasping of the sword arm, each was unarmed. So trust in the other person leads to trust in the situation, and opens the way for communication, not conflict. Trust in others also implies an optimism and a positive attitude, and so for effective channelling of effort and energy. Even the need for and trust in personal vitality is important, as anyone who has been ill for a while well knows, for it can be specially tiring to sustain a conversation when health and spirits are temporarily low.

The other prerequisite is an abiding interest in other people. Ideally conversation is a reciprocating, stimulating activity that enables us to know more about others and their situation, as they about us. And the sharing is usually more interesting and effective if it is similar to the interchange of melody and accompaniment in an orchestra, rather than a take-over of one-way traffic down a one-way street.

A main barrier to ease of conversation, however, can reside in the old bogey of shyness. Many people have experienced shyness during their lives, and so can be helpful in drawing out those afflicted. But it has also been pointed out that shyness, for various reasons, may be a form of 'I-ness,' and people can develop an ability to nurture conversation with others if they are willing to extend their own selves.

Conversation occurs at many levels in life, ranging from the brief social chat surrounding business meetings, to the often interesting exchange at informal social gatherings, to what can develop into a lively art in its own right at dinner parties. All occasions have, however, some elements in common, and a glance at these may help avoid a few pitfalls and replace them with some positive ideas.

The aim of the game is to find an interest in common; or a topic on which the other person is specially knowledgeable and is willing to talk, and so can tell you much that is fascinating which you might otherwise never know. It is a game that can take both parties, as it were, outside themselves, and that, played with skill and good fortune, can be greatly entertaining and refreshing. So when you feel tired and do not want to go out to a party or when you have invited friends in and half regret the idea, a happy amalgam of guests can lend magic to the occasion so that everyone leaves with a new perspective on life. In these times of prefabricated entertainment, when much that is tops in performance can be wired into the home, lively conversation can still offer a unique form of participation for everyone involved.

Between the hellos and the good-byes

As in our chapter on interviewing, the use of the spoken word in meeting people often pivots round the appropriate question. The first round beginning with the 'How are you?'s can be easily accomplished, and is rarely treated too seriously or leads to any great surprises. Then comes the stage of broad generalities which, if all else fails, can lead to the stand-by topics such as the weather and cricket on one side of the Atlantic, or the recent snowstorm or hockey game on the other.

But if social contacts and conversation are to widen, it follows that it is helpful to maintain an active interest in many events in life, from straight news, to current films, plays, and concerts, or to ballet and opera. While books are available everywhere, the art scene may also include special exhibits at galleries, libraries, and museums; and programmes of special interest on television. There is, in addition, the sports scene; and recently, with television bringing an abundance of coverage into the home, growing interest in the political arena.

Once you find a topic in common, you can keep the ball in air by responding and furthering the development of the idea through comment, perhaps leading to another query. As this leads out your partner, and the yeast of conversation begins to work, add a personal touch of your own opinion, so encouraging your partner to do the same. This not only furthers interest, but now both partners are also informing each other about themselves; and no matter what the knowledge and enthusiasm for a subject is, people are still the most fascinating topic in the world.

When people are really interested in something, they usually talk about it well; and while there are other areas which can provide potential material, their use should be tempered by a special awareness of response. Some people, for example, but not all, enjoy talking about their work; though it is an unwritten law of social exchange never to ask for professional, and so somewhat free, advice. And while it may be fascinating, people do not always enjoy talking about others in the same business. Similarly some younger people, but not all, enjoy talking about their future; and some older people, but not all, enjoy reminiscing. Within such categories you may strike gold, as hearing a scientist talk about new techniques, a young athlete about training for a special competition, or seventy-year-olds describing memories of grandparents, which may take you back over a century in time.

It can also be helpful to remember that everybody is a celebrity some-where, and regarded in a special, and let's hope not notorious, way at work, at home, at school or, because of a special hobby or skill, at a club. Open your ears and you can tap a sense of abiding interest when a fisherman describes his particular kind of absorption, a cook the creation of a special dish, or a musician the history of a particular instrument.

One aspect of the use of good words, well spoken which can happily occur in a social context, is the paying and receiving of compliments. Obviously they must be given and met with sincerity, avoiding the pitfall of over-emphasis or gush on either side. Yet everyone appreciates hearing the occasional something pleasant about themselves spoken with a genuine empathy and spontaneity. Such a sign of approval can act as a personal tonic in an often impersonal world, and may range from specific comment on the colour of a dress, the cut of a suit, or of flowers on a table or pictures in a room. A compliment can be given simply and easily, reflecting appreciation of a certain kind of care that goes into living.

But the giving requires its own kind of trust, for it is a gentle form of offering, and like presents, large or small, is most likely to be proffered in a climate of acceptance. Rejection on any scale is a tough school, and it is important that balancing words of thanks be spoken to complete the informal ritual. So to avoid any cutting of the flow of that section of the conversation, and without being effusive, it is helpful to try to what is sometimes called 'turn' a compliment. This can include a return phrase of continuity about the comment, adding perhaps your reasons for liking it, or a small anecdote about the choice involved.

In contrast, and as a possible antidote to some of the life-is-hard, life-is-earnest pressures of everyday work and living, an occasionally glorious game is played, known as the art of the happy insult. It is another form of signalling acceptance and can only be played where there is mutual trust and liking; otherwise, of course, taken seriously, it would lead down the path of social disaster. It may range from gentle teasing, which is often a sign of affection, such as the 'couldn't eat a thing' type of comment after an excellent meal, to the 'flattery will get you nowhere' putdown following an outrageous compliment. It often escalates from straight-face banter to winning score, which can be achieved through breaking-up and laughter or through rendering the other person speechless with happy indignation because they are unable to think of a final comment to cap the previous player.

This informal, yet potentially highly skilful word-play may be heard among a variety of in-groups among the arts, for example, or among teams in sports, or among teenagers. It needs a common background of experience and interest which gives a starting-point for reference and allusion, and often provides a safety valve for tilting at the windmills of influence and authority which somewhere, we feel, beset our lives.

If it can be said that any topic is taboo these days, there are a few that may be best avoided, and common sense and tact will indicate how far to pursue a conversation that could be difficult or sad for others. But while some topics, such as babies, or pets, or shop or office talk may be entrancing to both parties, they may also contain little that is new. So they can become repeats of well-worn grooves which, however interesting to the teller, may not always entertain the listener for long.

Which can lead us to consider how much time people spend actually talking with, rather than at, others. It seems a normal human failing that people sometimes need the reassurance of hearing themselves re-tell an anecdote, or place order in the world by airing a viewpoint. And occasionally, as in a difference of opinion, there may be need of the challenge to discover personal views and put them into words, along the lines of a question previously noted, 'How do I know what I think till I hear what I say?' In participating in any argument, there is however a useful skill which sometimes seems a gift of personality, but which can be nurtured; this involves listening carefully, so as to understand, though not necessarily agree with, other views. Here it is helpful if the voice sounds considerate rather than threatening, for any form of verbal or vocal bludgeoning is the opposite of vocal stroking.

Which, after all, is where we came in.

Voice routine

Continue as before, remembering your checkpoints prior to relaxation:

spine lengthen, neck free;
back widen, shoulders open.

- Review the work on vowel sounds, then refer them with greater awareness of their length and values to the rhyme-scheme in the following simple lyric:

Drink to me only with thine eyes,
    And I will pledge with mine;
Or leave a kiss but in the cup

And I'll not ask for wine.
The thirst that from the soul doth rise
  Doth ask a drink divine;
But might I of Jove's nectar sup,
  I would not change for thine.

From To Celia, Ben Jonson

If you speak such lines slowly and quietly, and with respect for their punctuation, the words will do much for you, and you cannot help but let through the imagery, flow, and spirit of the poem.

And now, in keeping with developing a sense of contrast, try the following lines with a sense of spontaneity:

I had a hippopotamus; I kept him in a shed
And fed him upon vitamins and vegetable bread;
I made him my companion on many cheery walks
And had his portrait done by a celebrity in chalks.

His charming eccentricities were known on every side,
The creature's popularity was wonderfully wide;
He frolicked with the Rector in a dozen friendly tussles,
Who could not but remark upon his hippopotamuscles.

If he should be afflicted by depression or the dumps,
By hippopotameasles or the hippopotamumps,
I never knew a particle of peace till it was plain
He was hippopotamasticating properly again.

From I Had a Hippopotamus, Patrick Barrington

Assignments

Unless having to combine a social with a business function, most people wish to relax and enjoy things without pressure of fulfilling a role other than being themselves. And since the atmosphere of a gathering is created by the personalities involved, it would be hard to create dry runs of value, particularly where initial moments of small talk are involved. There are, however, common elements involved in meeting people easily, such as the ability to respond to the thread of another's conversation, as well as to initiate ideas oneself, and to have the confidence to think quickly and express comments clearly and within range of another person's viewpoint. Just as some people write a letter to prepare the muscles of concentration for other forms of writing, so in a slightly different way you can explore some of the ideas in this chapter on improvisation, with a partner or in small groups in a class.

- Divide into partners A and B.
- A starts an anecdote such as 'something strange happened on my way to the library, or to work, or to school.'
- B interjects with a choice of only two comments: 'That's good' or 'That's bad.'
- Whichever the response, A does an about-face by continuing, 'No, it wasn't, because ...'

This takes mental agility and should be linked, if possible, with maintaining the thread of the story.

- After a few minutes, switch roles.
- Then try a variation in which B uses only such comments as 'No!' or 'You did?' or occasional 'Oh's, 'Ah's or 'U-uuh's.

In such a context these can be used to see how purely vocal response creates a flux of influence between listener and speaker, which will be investigated further in our final chapter.

To stretch the imagination, which as you will remember is one of the roots of reaching towards an understanding and so of communicating with, others, try improvising a whole series of conversations between contrasting objects, or between famous people from history, or between characters from different novels or plays.

Create your own ideas from the following examples, choosing what is familiar so that you speak from the viewpoint of what you know:

- Oil and vinegar, pen and pencil, adding machine and computer. Cat and mouse, horse and buggy, monkey and tree.
- Elizabeth I and Queen Victoria, Lincoln and Kennedy, Turner and Picasso.
- Sherlock Holmes and Hercule Poirot, Jane Eyre and Eliza Doolittle.
- Then improvize what happens when strangers start a conversation: while waiting for a job interview, or an exam; or when in a coffee bar or on a train; or during a delay at an airport.
- Then have the same people meet by chance, under similar circumstances in ten years' time. What has happened to them in the interim – have they gone up in the world, or down?

Part Three
Other People's Words

13
Reading Aloud

As with many walks of life, the world of speech could be said to be divided into two sorts of people. There are those happiest using their own words, and those happiest using other people's words. In the last section we concentrated on the first group, and now it is time to consider the second. Here we turn from a pattern of direct communication, or the personal challenge of the expression of ideas and choice of words, to interpretive communication, involving someone else's pre-selected means of expression.

So from various forms of speaking in public, we turn to reading aloud in public. Though the result should sound similar to any other form of speaking, here we try to re-enact the feelings and thoughts that led the author to choose his words. The aim is to ingest another person's expression by tuning ourselves to its origins and, with respect for its significance, to let it sound as if it rises from our own being. Or, as was once remarked about someone reading the Bible during a memorial service 'he read the lines as if they had come newborn out of his own mind.'

Reading aloud, when done with integrity, should not sound artificial, disjointed, or mumbled, so creating barriers for the listener who has no printed record in front of him. Rather it should have the same flow as everyday, connected speech, being another outerance, or extension of our usual delivery, thus joining the listener to our interpretation of the author's intent. The skills which aid our purpose include an imperceptibly quick, silent reading ahead, which is immediately blended into a reading aloud at sight. This, in turn, later forms the basis of prepared reading and, when required, of what is interestingly called learning, not by rote, but by heart.

Ideally, as suggested in our brief discussion of some of the differences between the written and the spoken word in Chapter 6, everyone can develop ability in reading either their own or other people's words aloud.

Understandably, however, we tend to fall into whichever camp seems easiest and suits our talent best. A natural public speaker, for example, who enjoys the flow of selection and organization, comments, 'I can say it myself, so it just seems harder to use someone else's words.' While a natural reader, who enjoys interpretation says, 'When you read aloud you don't have to think yourself of arranging what to say. It's done for you.'

Practice in conveying your own ideas, leading to the search for a widening means of expression and vocabulary, gives one kind of confidence. Experience in interpreting the written word gives another. Not only does it build an inherent variation in the catching and holding of listener response; it also gives the opportunity to breathe life into a vast range of human expression that would otherwise be conserved in the everlasting silence of print.

Here, to avoid misunderstanding later, comes a reminder that there are two kinds of print. First there is silent-writing: in the more private and involved communication of some poetry and novels, and in the factual writing of much journalism and many reports. Conversely there is 'speaking-writing,' which is resonant with the tunes and echoes of the human voice, such as all dialogue in plays or in stories, and most narrative and lyric poetry. It is important to accept that this difference, while obvious from one viewpoint, is easy to forget from another. Often less experienced readers will announce early in a course that they have 'really been practising this week,' and add with haloes shining that they combined their work with reading in other areas. Inquiry elicits that they read aloud the editorial of their daily paper, or their history or accounting text, or psychology notes. Such texts are fine in their way, but they are rarely intended for the orchestration of the human voice, and are more suited for consumption by the human eye.

For our purpose, we shall soon divide speaking-writing into two major divisions: informative and interpretive, both being regarded as equally important. For, although one may seem more relevant to the person in business or the sciences, and the other to the person interested in the arts, each will be found to stretch the reader's capability.

First, however, among the differences between silent reading, which most people feel they can do well, and reading aloud, which requires a separate talent, is that, in the former, interpretation occurs solely in the mind of the reader; and in the latter it occurs in the voice of the reader as well. In this lies part of the delight of being read aloud to; for much of what could be called the heavy work is done for us as the reader's voice explains the events, colours the characters, and maintains the thread of the narrative. We can sit back and enjoy the sound of the people and the mosaic of the situation, so having the fun without, as it were, the responsibility. We can also be reasonably mobile and pick up an occupation, such as ironing or woodwork, so leaving the imagination free to close the link between the author's intent and that magic world of the private theatre of the mind.

All such benefits can crumble like a house of cards, however, unless the reader can place absolute reliance on technical skills, so being free to concentrate on the imaginative aspects of an enthralling and demanding discipline.

The skills involved

EYE-SCANNING
Effective reading aloud has a vital prerequisite that involves an invisible, lightning-fast co-ordination between eye and brain and voice and speech. For those who need confidence in this matter, there is no alternative to steady, daily practice of ten to fifteen minutes a day, which may be needed for from three to six months.

The first requirement is the ability to look ahead. This is the pivot upon which all other factors depend, and the aim is so to free the eye that it eventually travels not with the word or two being spoken, but a half, and later a whole, line and more ahead. While the task is a grind, and will not initially sound anything like sense, there is an exercise which is now a must. It takes a leaf out of the book that says a similar ability is essential in music, and it is called the masking exercise.

- Be kind to yourself at the start by being sure to begin with a book that is written in speaking-writing, and that has reasonably large print and narrow pages. Have an envelope or note-pad handy with which to create the mask.
- Open the book anywhere, relax, and let the eye scan the opening line of any paragraph. As this occurs, aim to imprint the content on your memory. Because you may want to use muscular as well as verbal memory, since speech is a muscular action, you may notice that your tongue, lips, or jaw will tend to rehearse the process in quick, slight movements.
- Take your time, cover the line with the mask, and if possible looking up and towards imagined listeners, speak it aloud, aiming for no more at first than a smooth dictation speed. Provided there was no hesitancy, pause, relax, and scan the next line. Take your time, do a first memory-check if necessary then, when assimilated, look up, mask the line, and speak it.

Do not be dismayed if within these early trial runs there is occasional hesitancy. The exercise requires what is, to many, a totally new look-ahead synchronization of eye, memory and speech. Any such co-ordination requires great concentration, and this is unlikely to be totally consistent at first. Continue to maintain that even, measured, pace. Better by far to begin to be able to accomplish a paragraph steadily and surely by such means within a week, than to rush unevenly and give up within a few days.

Regular, conscience-clear practice at this, and gradually two things will begin to happen: a slow, but nevertheless dependable fluency, and a first growth of confidence.

- Now you can progress to perhaps smaller print and wider pages and, when all seems steady, increase the pace; keep, though, to a dictation speed.

Soon this look-ahead rhythm, instead of giving an initial, understandably stilted and broken result, will occasionally provide the confidence to go ahead, and you will find you can now give a semblance of meaning to sentences that run over two or three lines. This control will gradually extend to paragraphs and, very gradually, perhaps rather like those once-daring young men in their early flying machines, you may for a few seconds and then minutes achieve a sense of lift-off. Suddenly, instead of your eye being confined to within perhaps a couple of words of your speech, it has given you a new freedom.

You know what is coming; your mind has time to comprehend content easily and accurately, and so to pre-set voice and delivery according to the needs of whole sections of context. And you will find you can look up and include your listeners in the situation – not occasionally to stare them out of countenance, but so that they can see into your eyes, which are hopefully sympathetic to the situation. As in any form of public speaking, a glance can also give you an awareness of listener response.

HANDLING THE TEXT

As you begin to master this essential ability to read ahead, you can incorporate a few more points to help make your reading sound as much like speaking and as illuminating as possible for your listener.

- Hold the book up and slightly to one side, neither hiding it nor hiding behind it. This will enable you to look up occasionally, to keep your back and neck in good alignment, and to avoid any temptation to read

down and into the book rather than out and into the mind of the listener.
- Continue to maintain your new habit of looking ahead. Also, before starting, make time for a quick, speed-read pick-up of content and style. Take special note of opening and closing sentences so that if, as in much sight-reading, you are totally unfamiliar with a passage, you can forewarn and so forearm yourself for needs to come. It is vital that first impressions shall be clear to you if they are to make sense to the listener; and an awareness of his response will feed confidence back to you.
- Gain attention by giving the vocal signal for starting; use a pitch slightly higher than medium.
- Unless the ending is designed to leave a sense of doubt, mystery, or uncertainty, signal the end with a final downward inflection.

USE OF PUNCTUATION
Punctuation exists to help break a passage, through varying lengths of stop, into segments that will clarify meaning. When an author flicks in a comma, he indicates a slight division of meaning, usually accompanied by a strong sense of continuity. When he inserts a semi-colon, he points to a more extended division; and with a colon he indicates that a particular example, or often a list of facts, is coming. With a full stop or a period, he shows completion of a segment of meaning, and with a paragraph he indicates that a larger unit has been covered.

While this may seem obvious and elementary, lack of consideration for the author's marks is often a major technical factor in creating a negative experience for both reader and listener. Furthermore, although such pauses can add greatly to meaning, they require a certain confidence. While, when they work well, they can include many implications of thought and feeling, they can to many people unconsciously equate the awful gap of silence with the ultimate gap of death.

Unfortunately, except for people already gifted, the topic of reading aloud is rarely given responsible attention in education, and for many the faculty tends to disappear down the well of non-use. Recordings by actors and public figures may be utilized, and these can give an invaluable insight into plays, and into past and current events; but it is sad if they are a continual substitute for present voices that otherwise remain mute. For if language began as sound, how can people use it with any personal range, let alone write it, if they never try out and hear good examples from within their own bones? How can they share and enjoy such inheritance without need of any hardware or effects of any kind, except in simple and direct communion with the presence of others? Granted, it can be difficult for some, and it is always hard to struggle at something that for others seems a gift. But while reading aloud can rarely be improved without discipline and practice, it can be done with encouragement and with time.

There is need of a balanced attitude to the role punctuation plays in reading aloud. Just as attention must be paid to it when writing, it needs to be considered when re-sounding written material. For apart from the ladder of meaning suggested by the selection and arrangement of vocabulary and syntax, the punctuation of a piece is similar to the use of time-signature, bars, and phrases in music. To speak rough-shod through it, and without awareness of its contribution, is to ignore a vital means of conveying the full significance of a passage to a listener.

Here is another exercise which many people find helpful, for it takes into account the variety of both change and continuity in the author's thought, by giving particular value to his marks. Needless to say, like the masking exercise, it is done in slow motion at first, and should not be expected to sound like immediate sense. However, you will find that with time, and by retaining the principle yet making invisible use of the mechanics, interesting results can appear.

- Read a passage aloud, and with a good scanning action keep the eyes at least half to one line ahead. If you wish, record it on your own rough tape as your temporary control.
- Read the same passage aloud, but to it add a count-aloud of the following values for each punctuation mark: one for a comma, two for a semicolon, three for a colon, four for a full stop, and six for a paragraph.
- Read the passage again, this time making the counts silently but being absolutely sure to give each its full value. For here comes the crux of the matter: because you are giving a value similar to the author's for the change of lengths between the thought, you are also giving time for that thought to take place; and this applies as much to you as to your listener. As you give each stop its appropriate time, the subtlety of each change has room to be initiated in you as you interpret it to have taken place in the mind of the author, and you then have a fair chance of reflecting his thoughts and feelings as truly as possible in the sound-mirror of your voice.
- Repeat the last reading with a degree more flow, but retaining these time values in mind. If you wish, make a rough tape and compare it to your control reading.

Now that you are scanning ahead, thinking in tune with the author and out to the listener, your reading should begin to sound like the result of thought which you have personally digested. At the same time, you might find it useful to glance back to the section on the musical significance of sound in Chapter 4, with its reminder of the enrichment of words in their phrases through use not only of their image but of the complementary value of their sound. Hopefully there is now some development from a less personal, perhaps non-committed, previous delivery; and improvement can be nurtured by practice. There is no avoiding this factor, but provided it is backed by concentration and effort, letting technique develop rather than pushing it in any way, practice will over some months pay good dividends.

Finally, always remember your listener. While you are now beginning to add comment to your material, again arising from within and not imposed from without, it can be useful to bear in mind the response to this point of one student who suddenly beamed, 'Oh, I see what you mean. You gotta ponda longa!' While the pondering should not be overdrawn according to the needs of the action, that now infinitesimal pause coming from punctuation often provides the listener with a needed stretch of time. In addition, remember that sound takes longer to travel than sight; and the listener's only resource is your sound, for he has no recourse to the sight of the print.

Prepared reading and memorizing

It goes without saying that the above skills are the prerequisites of effective prepared reading, and of any memorization of a passage for speaking aloud. Before we discuss the more imaginative aspects of these two processes, we will take a brief look at some of the developments which can arise as an extension of these skills.

As we become more familiar with a passage, it can seem that the words, instead of becoming part of ourselves, appear to be veering off course. It can even seem that the reading lacks integrity as it appears to lose its initial spontaneity and leaves us frustrated with our own selves.

This can be because we try to finalize a 'how-to-say-it' plan of action before we have truly come to grips with all the implications of a passage and with what we feel and think about it. So the frustration is really a factor of internal decisions, and lack of these should not be mistaken for poor technique. 'My voice does not come out right' often expresses a result, while the cause lies in expecting too much of our resources too soon.

It is hardly surprising if that which is not yet ready to be expressed does not come out the same way twice. So wait until the roots are ready, and try to join them to that initial process of reading at sight. This is largely a matter of first-impression intuition, which gives a valuable because uncluttered response. For sometimes, as in 'a little knowledge is a dangerous thing,' the halfway house between a first reading and a thoroughly investigated piece of speaking from memory can be a disconcerting phase.

As to the skills of memorizing itself, there are few short cuts, though there is great variety in the time people need. There are apocryphal stories, for example, of a few actors in once-popular weekly repertory in England and in the equivalent summer 'stock' in the United States, who are such 'fast studies' that they are reputed to be able to take one and sometimes two silent read-throughs of their lines and then walk into rehearsal, or even out on stage, memory perfect. Most ordinary mortals, however, find memorization a slow process, but it is one, incidentally, that many people quietly pursue for private fascination and delight. For the best good words that are truly assimilated can accompany a traveller throughout life, and offer not only quiet comfort but, like relatives and friends, the discovery of new textures and perspectives every so many years.

The secret of developing memory lies, for most people, in a varying blend of concentrated attention on the sequence of the words and on their connecting associations, which may be deep within a passage. When the writing is good, containing a consistency, aptness, and rhythm that give form to the subject, the speaker may hardly be aware of the transition from not-knowing to not-sure to almost plugged-in; and this advance comes not just from the words but from, as it were, a sense of kinship with their origins in the author's thought.

This association with words tends to be among the reasons why actors enjoy playing in any of Shaw's plays, for they are so easy to study. And why many people find they quote so much from Shakespeare, for his words are so graphic and appropriate that they have become an intrinsic part of the culture of the language. Yet they seem to spring from mind to speech with a barely conscious need to memorize, and simply to be there because they are understood in the soul and in the bone.

A further point about what can be called committing words to memory comes when you have delved for their significance and searched for their connections. When you are beginning to have a glimmer of how you wish to utter, outer, and so share them with the birds, the bees, a class, an audience – or whatever – begin to sound them quietly. This can help their very orchestration for they can now weave a spell that you may, beyond all logic, be able to catch from the printed page as you bring them into being with your breath. This will give further dimension to memory, which in turn will begin to act as a sounding board for your intent.

Voice routine

Continue as before, making a special check of the relationship between head, neck, and shoulders.

- Keeping the shoulders easy, rotate the head slowly one way and then slowly the other.
- Let the chin drop, totally relaxed, on to the chest.
- Raise the head easily and slowly, as if lifting it by that piece of elastic to the ceiling.
- Repeat slowly, breathing out as the head drops, and in as you raise the head.
- Following rhythmic practice of vowel sounds combined with consonants, work on the following patter exercise:

The centipede was happy, quite
   Until the frog in fun, said –
'Pray, which leg goes after which?'
   Which worked her mind to such a pitch
She lay distracted in a ditch –
   Considering how to run.   Anonymous

Assignments

Check points noted in this chapter on reading aloud, with special reference to eye-scanning and looking ahead.

Try the exercise suggested on the use of punctuation while reading aloud, moving on to your own choice of passages. Meanwhile, in preparation for points in the following chapters, here is a passage to read aloud on two contrasting actors from lectures by a noted theatre director. Though we do not all wish to act, the descriptions are valuable not only for their comments on the integration of personality behind the spoken word, but also for the author's sense of exhilaration and adventure in the medium of the written word.

To reach an understanding of a difficult role, an actor must go to the limits of his personality and intelligence – but sometimes great actors go farther still if they rehearse the words and at the same time listen acutely to the echoes that arise in them.

John Gielgud is a magician – his form of theatre is one that is known to reach above the ordinary, the common, the banal. His tongue, his vocal cords, his feeling for rhythm compose an instrument that he has consciously developed all through his career in a running analogy with his life. His natural inner aristocracy, his outer social and personal beliefs, have given him a hierarchy of values, an intense discrimination between base and precious, and a conviction that the sifting, the weeding, the selecting, the dividing, the refining and the transmuting are activities that never end. His art has always been more vocal than physical; at some early stage in his career he decided that for himself the body was a less supple instrument than the head. He thus jettisoned part of an actor's possible equipment but made true alchemy with the rest. It is not just speech, not melodies, but the continual movement between the word-forming mechanism and his understanding that has made his art so rare, so touching and especially so aware. With Gielgud, we are conscious both of what is expressed and of the skill of the creator: that a craft can be so deft adds to our admiration ...

Paul Scofield talks to his audience in another way. While in Gielgud the instrument stands halfway between the music and the hearer, and so demands a player, trained and skilled – in Scofield, instrument and player are one – an instrument of flesh and blood that opens itself to the unknown. Scofield, when I first knew him as a very young actor, had a strange characteristic; verse hampered him, but he would make unforgettable verse out of lines of prose. It was as though the act of speaking a word sent through him vibrations that echoed back meanings far more complex than his rational thinking could find: he would pronounce a word like 'night' and then he would be compelled to pause; listening with all his being to the amazing impulses stirring in some mysterious inner chamber, he would experience the wonder of discovery at the moment when it happened. Those breaks, those sallies in depth, give his acting its absolutely personal structure of rhythms, its own instinctive meanings: to rehearse a part, he lets his whole nature – a milliard of super-sensitive scanners – pass to and fro across the words. In performance the same process makes everything that he has apparently fixed come back again each night the same and absolutely different.

I use two well-known names as illustrations, but the phenomenon is there all the time in rehearsal, and continually reopens the problem of innocence and experience, of spontaneity and knowledge.

From *The Empty Space*, Peter Brook

14
Reading Aloud:
To Inform and To Narrate

Practice in reading aloud all manner of speaking-writing is invaluable to those who wish to increase their effective use of words in any medium. It awakens voice and ear to nuances not always available when words stay mute on the page and so lack resonance in the mind; it increases openness to our own and to other people's expression of integrity because experience recognizes similar quality; it poses a continuing challenge of seeing if we can make what has been called the imaginative leap into different forms and styles; and through the need for adaptability it keeps us on our vocal toes, helping to avoid too many personal ruts or too set a manner of expression.

In opening our awareness of how we can gradually use our voices to say what we feel other people mean, we make a more perceptive use of ear training, which is in turn awakened to the impression we gain from other people's voices. By the example of reading other people's words aloud, we also enrich our own resources and develop the ability to express them, and thus gain confidence in the exploration of vocabulary. And somewhere along the line we develop an invaluable and built-in sense of the sound, in combination with the structure, of language. Then the topic of grammar, instead of seeming dry, divorced from and to some people an impediment to communication, can take on another dimension as part of a whole channel of sound and meaning.

Furthermore, what has been called an 'arrangement of parts' takes on additional significance, for since reading aloud must take the listener into account, room can be made for the subtle turning of meaning and feeling for the benefit of someone else. It is this factor which can sometimes be lost when people are primarily concerned with the privacy of the written medium, for it leads them to concentrate largely on content. This is fine for the printed page, but the interpreter who is reading aloud must re-conceive the material in such form and style to be of use to the receiver.

Now we are ready to turn to the first of the two major types of material useful for practice in reading aloud, which, because it is fundamentally concerned with the clarity of factual meaning, makes for an excellent, down-to-earth start.

Informative reading aloud

Informative reading aloud must convey information clearly and with interest and, according to the situation, will require some degree of comment. (For just as the brisk words 'No comment' on the media from a politician are usually conveyed without expression, so conversely most phrases are used with a more positive outlook on life and are given suitable degrees of variety to convey meaning.) Naturally, vocal comment changes according to purpose, and this may range from reading aloud announcements, newscasts, or sportscasts, to doing a voice-over on commercials, or reading the minutes of the last meeting, or reading to children or to the blind; and it may sometimes include quotations from other sources in giving a speech or a report, or a lecture or sermon.

Confidence and accuracy are essential within any such situation, and mumbling, uncertainty, or inaudibility are out, for people need to be able to hear in order to understand and to remember what has been said. As with all use of the spoken word, clear thinking and consideration for the listener are prerequisites, for the voice must supply an interested channel for the material, avoiding any impression of boredom or of indifference, or over-involvement or of vocal embroidery.

A proportion of the range of examples listed above is concerned with reading aloud on the media and at public gatherings, where a microphone can ease any concern for audibility. Otherwise it is sad how, at some meetings, minutes and prepared reports are often given with more of a private mumble than a reading with any consideration for the key word – aloud.

It can be helpful to remember a number of factors in conveying information. For example, what is worth hearing is worth saying, so give your material the conviction to carry the content. When practising try to allow for necessary projection and to add a shade more variety than you normally would on your own – as if someone were at a distance from you instead of in the chair facing you.

Let it be personable, that is attractive or well-sounding, without being overly personal or individual, so that your voice and delivery become a carrying wave to serve the message clearly. Above all, take your time. You are probably giving a prepared reading and, while you know the facts, your listeners do not. Divide the facts somewhat, as in our previous discussion of punctuation, allowing slightly longer pauses for particularly detailed material than you normally would. You are assisting your listeners up the ladder of a certain meaning, and if you do it effectively and they are good listeners, they should be able to pass on accurately the gist of what you have said to others.

If you need to be doubly sure, check their retention by asking for a recap. For a real problem in communication can lie in the assumption that merely because something has been said, even as simply as possible, it has been understood and remembered within the context intended.

Interpretive reading

We are going to begin this topic, which covers narrative, poetic, and dramatic forms of speaking-writing, with mention of another age-old problem. This occurs when the reader says, 'I can hear it inside, but it doesn't seem to come out right,' and occasionally adds, 'Everything I read seems to sound the same.'

Let us aim for the right track with one golden rule: do not at any time ever, or even hardly ever, indulge in the idea of 'putting expression in.' This can result in a tendency to artificiality that once gave speech training an unfortunate reputation. Coupled with the need to project without the availability of microphones, the result was often twice false: in embryo and in enlargement. Indeed the less fortunate aspects of the school of elocution, or speaking out, evolved as if the speaker were standing underneath the potted palm emoting, fit to bust, 'The boy stood on the burning deck / Whence all but he had fled.' Unfortunately this worst form of amateurism was death to the true function of joining listener to author's intent, and it became a travesty of the very thing speech is intended to do. In other words, if the speaker's ego becomes more important than the words, it is likely to upset the whole applecart of their content.

This is not to suggest that interpretation of someone else's words need negate the speaker's personality, since this forms the highway of their journey. Rather it is a question of priorities: the word being primary, the speaker secondary; the aim being to enlighten the listener's mind and heart.

The narrative form

By form in this sense is meant the medium into which the author pours his intent and, obvious as this reminder may seem, it is important to give it respect. An imbalance can occur, for example, if an inexperienced speaker attempts to 'act' the narrative or lyric forms, or if the dramatic form lacks the essential grasp of character and conflict.

The narrative form includes the novel, the short story, and children's stories, and its needs are as varied as literature itself. The main element lies in the momentum of events which give line to the author's theme, and in the atmosphere and flavour of his style. Bearing in mind the points mentioned under the heading of sight-reading, the key lies in accurate eye-scanning, so that you can then use every imaginative hint that occurs. Use it as the basis of that relish of words we discussed in Chapter 4 under 'Musical significance of sound,' remembering that mind and heart must maintain that leap ahead within the author's world; as you believe, so the listener can believe through you.

In reassembling the experience beneath the words, sometimes in the theatre called the sub-text, a concentration of energy without tension is required so that, as action and description maintain momentum, the reader very quickly sees, hears, tastes, touches, and, if necessary, savours the content in advance. There are no half-way measures. This is why technique has to be dependable; and although it is only human to stumble occasionally, should this occur it is helpful, as with the actor who loses a line, to maintain the frame of mind, so aiming to give the listener as uninterrupted a picture of events as possible.

We have already discussed the value of taking careful, but not eventually obvious, note of the author's punctuation. And now comes a valuable factor which many readers use naturally: a sense of directing the listener's attention, as does the director in the theatre, to what is important. This is achieved not by emphasis in terms of giving a weightier sense to some sections, but rather by a subtle blend of those elements which modulate or change delivery (see Chapter 5). It is helpful if these are rooted in your quick comprehension of the twists and turns of the author's line, so that you are virtually following or accompanying his lead rather than taking conscious decisions yourself.

Thus the inexperienced reader is sometimes puzzled that, while he feels sure his interpretation is sincere, it seems as if everything he reads can sound similar and a bit ploddy. Although an analysis of the result might lead to the conclusion that, for example, more variety of pace is needed, the cause may lie in lack of flexibility in following the author's intent.

It is not often consciously realized that it is unnecessary to give every phrase equal value. Should this occur, the listener is left to do much sorting of material for himself instead of enjoying the pleasure of having it done for him. And since we do not speak in even phrases, but are continually trying to edit the cross-currents of the whirls and eddies of thought inside ourselves, it sounds extraordinarily unnatural, even in the planned expression arising from writing, if the spoken word suddenly becomes even and unspontaneous. To draw analogies with other arts, it would be similar to viewing a painting that lacked highlight or shadow, reading a writer who crosses every 't' and dots all the 'i's of meaning, or listening to somebody over-explain a joke.

The sight-reader needs to 'intuit' what is valuable and what is not, and in this he is also guided by what are virtually the signals of parenthesis. These are indicated by a rising inflection before the punctuation marks, which may be commas, dashes, or brackets. The pitch is usually lowered and the pace quickened within the marks. A rising inflection at the last mark then brings the meaning back to approximately the same pitch as that used before the paranthesis. With these signals in mind the reader seems to be saying subliminally to the listener, 'listen carefully to this,' 'that is not quite so important,' 'forget the other,' and 'note how this section is connected to that.'

Finally we come to the handling of dialogue in narration. Without being laboured, this must be suggested from within a strong visual and aural sense of the characters involved. Here again flexibility is vital, since the reader's voice may be needed to convey a wide range of people of vastly different backgrounds and ages, from men and women of every type and kind to all manner of children and condition of animals.

In addition to such variety, which comes not from 'putting on a voice' which usually has the tension of caricature, but from within the roots and connections of each person as supplied by the author, there is also need for the listener to know exactly when you are back in the third person, or narrative form, again. So you require vocal room for a minimum of both antagonist and protagonist, and possibly others, along with the accustomed and probably middle level of the story line. Here it is helpful to indicate the inside of quote marks with an infinitesimal, wait-for-it pause which, by the nature of its break and lift from the introduction into the dialogue, will signal that something different is coming. But there are times, however, when three or four brief lines of dialogue may need to be given on one breath, since they could come within one phrase or whole segment of the author's thought.

When these points have fallen into mind and heart from the text, one further consideration can be extended to the listener. Unless a story is being read aloud on radio, there is a strong complementary factor involved in the visual element of the reader's eyes and face. As we know, this can be used by looking up and towards, but not directly at, the listener occasionally. To convey character when using dialogue, it can also help to look slightly off-centre and to one side, as if actually addressing the other person involved. This can become particular fun when an adult, for example, is addressing a child and with the diagonal glance also looks down somewhat; and if the child takes the opposite diagonal and looks slightly up. All of which uses a convention that can appear completely natural, and will help give the listener a clear understanding of who is talking to whom, and when.

Voice routine

Continue as before

Assignments

Check the points noted in this chapter.
- For informative reading aloud, either compose your own announcements or contact a local radio or television station. Ask if you could
  have copies of past weather forecasts, community announcements, commercials, or news and sports events.
- Similarly, compose minutes of previous meetings of clubs or organizations; and create and read aloud announcements as for school, college,
  or church.
- When you feel you are making these readings clear, easy to remember,
  and free from mumble or artificial stress, and when you think you
  sound like talking rather than reading, record a few on your rough tape.
- When these are going well, add a couple to your major tape.

Make a practice of reading aloud good narrative work, especially by good storytellers and those who use dialogue. Dickens and Thackeray give wonderful comments on character and event, and they wrote in the days when reading aloud was an accepted custom. Cut your teeth on the classic short novel, *A Christmas Carol*. Read aloud to children, and you should begin to feel your voice can give extra dimension to the stereoscopic characters in *The Wind In The Willows* by Kenneth Grahame or, for people of all ages, *Watership Down* by Richard Adams.

Remember there is a continuing source of good words to be spoken aloud in so much that was written up to and including the times of Shakespeare. The oral tradition gives resonant expression to Chaucer's *Canterbury Tales*, and to the King James' version of the Bible. Here is part of a clause from Magna Carta, translated from the Latin of the legible copy in the British Museum. Note the absence of legal jargon, and that, if you look after the punctuation, the long phrases look after themselves.

Since we have granted all these things for God, for the better ordering of our kingdom, and to allay the discord that has arisen between us and our barons, and since we desire that they shall be enjoyed in their entirety, with lasting strength, for ever, we give and grant to the barons the following security:

The barons shall elect twenty-five of their number to keep, and cause to be observed with all their might, the peace and liberties granted and confirmed to them by this charter.

If we, our chief justice, our officials, or any of our servants offend in any respect against any man, or transgress any of the articles of the peace or of this security, and the offence is made known to four of the said twenty-five barons, they shall come to us – or in our absence from the kingdom to the chief justice – to declare it and claim immediate redress.

From *Magna Carta*

15
Reading Aloud:
The Poetic and Dramatic Forms

The poetic form

The poetic form of verse gives expression to experience beyond the boundaries of everyday logic and connection. Being a transcending, heightened,
and often highly compressed and occasionally intricate form, it neither reads
nor sounds like everyday speech. Yet the art of speaking verse lies in giving
resonance to the words in such a way that the speaking illuminates meaning
and feeling without artificiality.

As with everyone concerned with interpretation, the verse-speaker is a
joiner, and because his personal resources are not the same as those of other
speakers, his vision is individual, and no one person can tell another exactly
how to give sound to a poem. But it can be helpful to take into account some
of the differences within the poetic form, as between narrative, lyric, and
dramatic verse, if the listener is to gain enrichment. And one of the
differences between verse and prose, although it does not always appear in
modern verse, is an extended and more regular use of the comforting quality
of rhythm. While, as we have already discussed, this occurs to a degree in
most good prose and is indeed the mainstay of any art, poets in particular use
it as an intrinsic part of momentum and significance. And, hopefully, this is
how it will be used by the speaker; not as a thump-ti-tump and noticeably
overrriding wallop, but as a barely noticeable foundation to sound, sense,
and structure. This echoes a point raised in previous chapters about things
being IWBN – in without being noticeable.

While there are many variations of rhythmic pattern in English verse, one
that is of particular value for the speaker to experience is the series of five
short-long bars, as it were, of blank verse. This is not only fundamental to
many great lyric poems, but is also used with many variations in Shake-

speare's plays. And while not everyone wishes both to speak verse and to be able to act, the one is a marvellous foundation to the other. For when the time comes to use the voice within the extra dimension of character, the means of breathing and phrasing and a sense of the choreography and musicality of words are there, waiting to be tapped.

A major difference between much verse and prose is in the use of rhyme: that dependable, quiet satisfaction afforded by the repeat, with variation, of similar sounds at expected intervals at the ends of words. If the poet has included this feature within his form, the listener should have access to it; and in giving value to its harmonics there is again need of balance: between ignoring it on the one hand and overdoing it on the other. Naturally speakers develop their own way of using this device, but many find it helpful to think of rhyme as a bell within that inner ear which gives a sense of control to the voice. It is as if, while part of the mind continues to think and feel ahead, another part aims to carry over the like sound until it is met by the matching sound a line or more later. In a sense, the use of rhyme is similar to the resolving of harmony through chords of appropriate keys in music. As can be imagined, retaining the inner echo and expectancy at the same time as concentrating ahead, possibly on the introduction of a further rhyme, is no small feat and requires a special openness to the full significance of the poem.

To point out this feature to the listener, there can be a small dwelling on similar syllables; this results in a slight stretch of time which occurs as indicated by the line down the page, thus giving visual as well as aural harmony to the poem. Such a holding back is reasonably simple when a pause at the end of a line is determined by punctuation. But when there is no punctuation, the speaker may use what is interestingly called a suspensory pause. This is the slight upward lilt denoting continuity which, coupled with the above stretch on the word, provides a near half-beat of syncopation before swinging on round with the sound and the sense to the next line.

While much verse, and particularly blank or unrhymed verse, is written continuously down the page, the majority of poems are given the structure of different verses, which are usually, but not always, the poet's equivalent of the paragraph. It is surprising how tempting it is to continue on down and ignore the signal of this break in terms of the shape of the poem and the author's intent. As with charging through other forms of punctuation, the loss of each pause is also a loss in significance; and even when great impetus is required to carry the sense forward, brief recognition of the end of the verse can be given with a slight change of pitch for the next.

One of the earliest forms into which people poured their stories, legends, and often their music, was the ballad or a narrative form. This was an intrinsic part of the oral tradition, having a simple line, rhythm, and rhyme; was good to say and easy to learn; and in many cases was often an early form of news sheet. Indeed right up to the expansion of literacy in Victorian times, ballads were an essential part of bar-room and parlour entertainment. In recent years, folk-singers have given new life to this form. But it can be tempting to poke fun at some outdated, or even classical ballads, by so thumping them out that they become tedious and seemingly immature. But a traditional ballad, spoken in the spirit intended, carries an ageless flavour because to survive it had to be simple and it had to be liked. It has long stood the ultimate test of being echoed within the memory of generations, and there is no higher credit than that.

Lyric verse is used to express a more romantic train of thought and feeling; while it too requires its own momentum, it also needs a special affinity for the blend of significance behind the words. In short, to serve them with all appropriate savour of the sweetness and sadness of love, friendship, and even life given and lost. Seen, not with immediacy and through someone else's eyes, as in acting, but viewed through that half-distance away that enriches our being through the ability to recollect experience in tranquility. Commit your integrity to the words, and they will give something back to you; or, as Shelley said in his 'Ode to the West Wind' (and there's a piece of speaking for you), 'Make me thy lyre, even as the forest is ...'

The sonnet is perhaps the most beautifully integrated expression of thought and feeling that exists in language. It is a case in which form and meaning are closely related, and the structure has to be brought out by the speaker. The compression of a major concept complemented by minor points takes careful assimilation and great concentration over the fourteen lines.

In contrast, modern or free verse sets its own challenge, since it is necessary to retain the spirit of often highly individual expression; and though close to the contemporary idiom, even when conveying complex thought it must approximate to the sound of everyday speech.

All these forms can require a most adaptable technique on the part of the reader. Such variety of words may need expression within the intimacy of radio or television, within the sense of enlargement needed in a classroom, or through projection of voice and image required in a hall or theatre.

The dramatic form

We now come, with some degree of readiness, to the interpretation of the dramatic form, involving the use of the spoken word as representing the thoughts, feelings, and whole psyche of a human being other than ourselves; and all within the many varied conditions of production and performance. Among the often indiscernible qualities that an actor requires are a vast pool of imagination, a knife-keen and intuitive awareness of other people in sound and in action, and a subtle response to an author's words in the form of dialogue. As conducted by a director, his entire being forms a unique instrument, for unlike other artists who play the piano or fashion material such as paint or stone outside themselves, the actor relies solely on his personality, voice, and physique to form a bridge between author and audience.

In a sense, the actor becomes an embodied extension of the verse-speaker and the storyteller who evoke people, places, and events simply with the voice. And he requires an innate ability to work, not solo in harmony with a text, but as an intrinsic part of the total plan of a production, in concert with others in the cast and with all the technicians and staff involved.

It is another of those tall orders, and one which makes similar demands even upon actors of widely differing backgrounds. For whether one is amateur or professional, in college or in school, the challenge is the same: to help enrich the lives of an audience through a completely believable version of a character created for this one production. Believable, in that the actor needs absolute commitment to whatever length and type of role he is portraying; created once, in that every production has the potential for creating a totally credible world that will never, ever, as in our early quote from Martha Graham, be the same 'in all time.' Yet out of the ephemeral temporality of action, other human beings can carry a vivid memory that stays with them for life, which gives proportion to the realities of their own existence.

Naturally, levels of performance vary with experience, and while it is true that acting cannot be taught as such, any more than any other art, an actor can develop his potential by keeping his total instrument as flexible and as open to the combined suggestion of director, author, and his own resources as possible. All of which must be pared down to the evocation he gains from and gives to the words of the text. These give him both the inner thoughts and the outer parameters of the character he is about to create, and all this takes more than a little homework.

Apart from attendance at rehearsals, time is necessary for a considerable delving into resources. These can include the background and foreground of the play and the life and times of the author, and a number of questions that the actor can ask in relation to the function and development of his character. Such detail is beyond the confines of a text such as this, and there are many excellent books which deal with such needs alone. (The interested reader should also refer to the author's companion text, *A Handbook of the*

*Theatre**, with particular reference to Chapters 2 and 6, 'The Director' and 'The Actor'; for while all chapters are related to the responsibilities of those involved in the production of a play, these two should be studied for the interrelationship with each other and with the whole.)

One focus that is important within our frame of reference, however, is to avoid thinking in terms of setting feelings and concepts about a character too soon. As in our section on preparing your own words for giving a speech, try to give the background some study, and to work on the sub-text, or the thoughts-behind-the lines, until your impressions have time to percolate. Aim to wait until an inner voice and vision begin to give intermittent echoes of the person you are seeking. For a character can be neither a copy of any one being, nor a creation totally divorced from other human beings. Since it is often suggested that an actor is, by virtue of his own resources, part-author of every character he creates, allow time for a depth of approach.

Soon this unique person may begin to speak to you from within the lines, but remember that it is rare for him to fall into place in one complete and rounded image. Listen for him, and always, always listen on his behalf to other characters, using this as much within your early preparation as during actual performance. Listening is as much an integral part of your dialogue as the actual words you speak, being an intrinsic part of the action; for the character's inward thoughts, often arising from other people's words and actions, will constantly give rise to what he says and does next.

Listening is also an absolute must in all situations that give rise to comedy, which, it should be remembered, needs to be viewed from within the character. The predicament is usually as serious for him as it is proportionately funny/amusing for an audience. Let the anchor of concentration go and two things can happen. (1) The actor peeks through and subconsciously turns the delivery of an audience-funny line into a consciously-funny line; for the voice is so wise and subtle an instrument that it momentarily lacks the truth of the character, and the laugh is lost. (2) The very spontaneity that creates or responds to the turns of surprise that are an essential part of comedy is also lost, and again the voice in its wisdom carries an nth degree of flatness – which would be like seeing a bubble of champagne fail to reach the top of the glass.

You can also let listening, in the sense of your own ear training, give a sense of control to your performance in that, if your character is about to be mad, glad, or whatever, there is nearly always a progression towards that

---

* Gage Educational Publishing, Toronto, Ontario, 1964; Heinemann Educational Books, 1973, paperback edition, 1980.

emotional state; and indeed the whole shape of a role must be tempered by varying degrees of intensity, of which you need to be aware if you are to build on and successfully repeat your interpretation.

Apart from inward and outward listening, one of the few golden rules in the apparently invisible art of acting is to let sensation precede action. Obvious as it may seem, if the dialogue indicates that you enter because you have lost something, look for it as you come and let the sense of loss predetermine what you say, and the reason predetermine how you say it. Or if a line is as simple as 'Oh, what a lovely day,' the sense of the day in all simplicity of significance for the character, of weather, grass, green, sun, air, sky, people, or what-have-you, must precede the words.

For herein lies an interesting factor about the voice. It is, if we will let it be, an amazingly true mirror of ourselves, or of our character's self, in action. Not only can it be used in real life for identification, and as such has already been allowed as evidence in law, it can also, as mentioned earlier, tell much about our mental and physical health; and in some space programmes it is part of the evaluation of potential candidates for performance during stress. It is also, as we know, created by muscular movement, and when movement is true, we usually say it looks right; in the case of vocal movement, during which the listener has no direct sensation and feel of control, we can only evaluate in terms of result, or the hearing-feeling, of the sound. So that when a line comes openly, with full conviction and with the appropriate resonance and harmonics arising from a well-tuned voice, it may be said to 'ring' true. And this is the quality of being on-line with the character that the actor must understand and equate with every on- and off-stage moment – from before the curtain rises to often long after it has come down.

Another general element within our context is that of accents of speech, already mentioned in an everyday-life context in Chapter 5, and this can lead us to the whole question of intelligibility versus reality in performance. The guideline here turns upon the need of all arts to be, in reality, artificial; the skill being in the artifice or technique that transcends illusion into belief. A large proportion of illusion also lies in the power of suggestion, and in this case in the ability of the actor to invoke words with such magic that an audience virtually leans forward to connect the circuit of response.

Because the actor must communicate or perish, it is important to remember that it is not merely for his character to think great thoughts and feel all manner of emotions; but also for the actor to create that slight gap between illusion and reality that the audience actually works to fill, helping to create its own insight and understanding of the character, the play, and the situation. The art of acting is thus concerned with an extension of belief. It is a matter of suggesting on the basis of truth, and not merely of being; which bogs a performance down on the treadmill of actuality, tends to separate roles, and makes it hard for a director to co-ordinate the production in the version conceived for that particular occasion.

The same applies to accents on stage, which must be based on a true inner hearing of the whole culture and mannerisms of what will be regarded as a different form of speech. But, while bearing in mind that a Scottish accent will not sound like an accent in a performance given in that part of the world, its use would probably have to be tempered in other regions such as London or New York, where the impact could be so strong as to prevent understanding, and could also attract attention to itself so that audience concentration on other and more important matters could be broken.

In the case of an accent of another language, the same concept applies. The result needs to be based on a true inner memory which keeps an actor on-line and un-phoney, suggesting rather than simply copying the original sound. The important element here is an adaptation of individual sounds so as still to carry the sense, and to it adding the melody, rhythm, and lilt from another culture, which will have a concomitant impact on the usual flow of connected speech.

Finally, with the spoken word, remember that the gathering of resources behind whatever evocation is required takes varying degrees of enthusiasm; for all communication takes a surge of energy to activate response; and in the case of speaking, the surge equates the never-ending catalyst of spontaneity.

Voice routine

Continue as before, occasionally staying relaxed on the floor from your preparation into exercises.

Use the following lines (a continuation of those in the routine following Chapter 6) to help you find a relaxed state. Be sure that you are in tune with the spirit of the words before breathing sound into them.

Here are cool mosses deep,
And through the moss the ivies creep,
And in the stream the long-leaved flowers weep,
And from the craggy ledge the poppy hangs in sleep.

From *Song of the Lotus Eater*, Tennyson

Then, as an experiment, try the lines again, but using the vowel sounds only. Naturally, 'ere are oo o'e eee,' is going to sound a bit strange, but if you can get the hang of it throughout the lines, and then occasionally take any lyric work in this way, it will help to give you an intrinsic feeling for the orchestration of words. In addition to pointing the rhyme, it gives a sense of the flow of the rhythm and the contrast between the long and the short vowels. It also helps to appreciate how the continuity of the resonance of vowels provides the underlying flow of feeling; while the stops, or consonants, break a passage into meaning. Then the aims, such as flexibility and control, in the previous exercises can better be used to balance sound in the service of intent.

Here, in contrast, is a quickie as reminder for the continuing need to develop range by exploration of contrast:

Silence in the gallery,
Order in the pit,
The people in the boxes
Can't hear a bit.   Anonymous

This can be taken by a group as a form of musical round. Or give a line to each speaker, always keeping to the rhythm.

– Play with it – let the voices juggle and catch it.
– Change the order of the last word in the first three lines, without prior discussion, and see if following speakers are fast enough in their response to complete the whole in a different order.

Assignments

Check the points noted in this chapter, and read aloud a sonnet of your own choice, or start with Shakespeare's 'Shall I compare thee to a summer's day?' which can be found in the complete works or in countless collections.

Note the rhythm, the chording of the rhyme, and where you will need a suspensory pause to denote a run-on line. Above all, and especially initially, take time to experience the images before voicing them. To make comparison with the day, visualize the person you feel is involved, and weigh the subtle difference in texture and meaning between the comparisons of 'lovely' and 'temperate.' This cannot be achieved by the immaturity of stress, but by delving inside the quick significance of the description. Look at the way meaning is conveyed by contrast, and right from the beginning take aim, as a slow-motion arrow in the air, for the conviction of the final couplet. Eventually treat the whole lightly and, with the impetus of delight, give it wings.

When it comes to the dramatic form of reading aloud, to many people the eventual goal is to take a character through from initial readings into performance. But reading aloud is also a challenging and fascinating way for everyone to become familiar with as wide a range of dramatic literature as they like to explore.

It can make a satisfying experience if everyone reads round, simply taking each character as the dialogue comes, whether the voice belongs to man, woman, child, or animal; consistency may vary initially, but because everyone contributes there can be a great sense of participation. It is also an effective means for everyone involved to develop a feeling not only for the sound and style of the various characters, but also for echoes of the voices of many playwrights.

The individual reader can explore a tremendous range of personal capability, and those specially interested should read aloud every character in a one-act play each week, or a three-act play every two or three weeks.

Whatever the circumstances, include some verse by Dylan Thomas, and in particular read aloud from his play for voices, *Under Milk Wood*. The sixty-three characters can be read by as few as six people; or for the sheer challenge of variety try a reading, not perhaps for public consumption, taking every role yourself. Listen to the slow litany of Bessie Bighead as she does the evening milking:

Peg, Meg, Buttercup, Moll,
Dan from the Castle,
Theodosia and Daisy,

as the chorus adds a benediction, and in five sentences utters a lifetime:

They bow their heads.
Look up Bessie Bighead in the White Book of Llareggub and you will find the few haggard rags and the one poor glittering thread of her history laid out in pages there with as much love and care as the lock of hair of a first lost love. Conceived in Milk Wood, born in a barn, wrapped in paper, left on a doorstep, big-headed and bass-voiced she grew in the dark until long-dead Gomer Owen kissed her when she wasn't looking because he was dared. Now in the light she'll work, sing, milk, say the cows' sweet names and sleep until the night sucks out her soul and spits it into the sky. In her life-long love light, holily Bessie milks the fond lake-eyed cows as dusk showers slowly down over byre, sea and town.

From *Under Milk Wood*, Dylan Thomas

16
Hearing in General and Listening in Particular

The sense of hearing

It is estimated that we spend well over half our communicating lives listening to other people's words, and for a number of reasons there is a lot more to the process than literally meets the eye. Being primarily connected to hearing, listening is dependent on the most deep-seated of our five special senses, and because we live in a world that is virtually a sonic fishbowl, stimuli are never-ending from birth to death; hearing being, in fact, the last of our senses to leave us.

It is also the hardest to shut off, for hearing is an integral part of our warning system and, should a particularly unpleasant sound occur, can take two hands in a usually unsatisfactory attempt. This is worth comparing to one hand to hold the nose against an unpleasant smell; or easy disposal of an unpleasant taste, fast withdrawal from a touch that burns, or shutting the eyes to a sight that repels.

Hearing involves no specific response such as the sniff, the grimace, or the 'ouch!'; though we may blink, or close the eyes in dread or in surprise at an occasional appalling noise. It may include an emergency turn of the head so that we can see and face the cause of danger; though sometimes the stimulus is so frightening that the response is to freeze; and when control over movement does return, it can lead to flight.

The sense of hearing, also interconnected with that of balance, is closely integrated with the brain for acceptance or rejection of all the sounds that impinge upon it; and, as we have discussed briefly under the heading of ear training, for control of our own vocalizing, as well as for perceiving other people's sounds and words.

As hearing provides the intake of the spoken word, which is our primary means of expression and exchange of ideas, it is also a vital link in our thinking process. Among the frustrating aspects of deafness is not just that the sensory deprivation of much of the taken-for-granted ease of conversation and the beauty of the special sound of music, and indeed of some speaking voices, may be lost, but that it is so easy for others to assume that deafness implies slowness of mind.

The brain helps us to interpret what we hear by the act of listening. For to hear is simply to perceive the invisible but vibrating waves of sound; but to listen is to give them our attention, and to make out of them a meaning that is new and enlightening, or accustomed and accepted. Thus there are countless vibrations that we make no attempt to translate further in any way, and awareness of these is minimal; you are likely to find many examples of this when making a recording for assignments in this book. Unless you happen to use it in a soundproof room or studio, playback will often bring to conscious recognition an abundance of continuous stimuli, which may include traffic noise, planes, wind, rain, or other people moving about.

A simple experiment can also indicate how people differ in their levels of awareness. If you ask a group, say of over twelve in number, to close their eyes and concentrate on such background sounds, you will usually find that there is far from agreement in the responses. Leaving thirty to sixty seconds between each suggestion, start, for example, by asking everyone to become aware of sound outside the building, then inside the building, and then inside the room. Some will notice dogs barking, a few voices, and a jet landing at a distant airport; others, in addition, someone whistling, a car door slam and/or the whir of machinery, and the sound of running feet. There can be similar variation in the receptivity to inside sounds, and if this happens when we are giving careful attention to our sonic world, it gives some indication of the varying range of our everyday awareness.

But because sound is the most primordial and invading of our senses, it is to some people the most terrifying. Especially when we hear something we do not understand, as during the first seconds of a sensation which we cannot label, so that we temporarily inhabit that gulf of experience to which we can give no name. Similarly it can also be the most heart-rending, for human beings in anguish can often make no word-sense of their experience; and our response is often likewise at the deepest level of communication. Within this context, it is noticeable how, in television newsreels of people caught in the agony of battle or natural disaster, the awfulness of their word-cries are usually covered by music or by voice-over commentary. It is interesting to conjecture what would happen if all the enormities of violence, presented live in the living-room, were to be given the same aural, as they currently are visual, impact. If this were done responsibly and not sensationally, it might compel more compassion into action.

It seems that light waves keep us that one bit removed from experience, as does the silence of print compared to the sound of words. For heard experience becomes shared experience; light waves capture life externally; sound waves embody life internally. Light is thereness and thenness; sound is hereness and nowness.

Varying forms of energy transmitted through vibration provide the physical sources of communication; and, while these are beneficial in many ways, they can be unpleasant or even deadly in others. Sound waves in extremis can lead to madness. One of the most interesting examples in literature is in the late Dorothy L. Sayer's classic about a man virtually murdered by being locked in a belfry during the ringing of the peal known as the 'Nine Tailors' (also the title of the novel), which was responsible for breaking his eardrums. And it is of interest that a major difference between sound and noise is that the latter, having vibrations of irregular frequency, is literally and physically less pleasing than the vibrations of regular frequency of the former. So much so that, in an experiment in ESP in Russia, a room filled with people was cleared within twenty minutes with no audible signal, but simply by irregular and uncomfortable vibrations.

Small wonder that there is occasional happy talk about good and bad 'vibes.' But transpose that into listening to some unpleasant and so harsh or grating voices, and it is easy to see how the response is automatically to tune out and/or turn away. An interesting point being: is the harshness a true manifestation of the personality, or is it the way the speaker has responded to life, so using the self and voice that together they appear to occupy a strident corner from which to bark back at the world?

As a final point under our present heading, it can be interesting to bear in mind that we cannot physically turn off the sense of hearing as we can the tap of other stimuli. So, while subliminal advertising in the visual sense can be banned, subliminal listening can never be. The former, as you will remember, is the kind of advertising which on television can be projected on to the screen so fast that it is perceived without conscious recognition and yet is still subconsciously received by the brain. In a listening sense that could be the equivalent of sleep-learning, whereby a piece of study, played on a tape-recorder with a small speaker under the pillow, is said to filter into the sleeper's mind and be ready for retrieval in the morning.

Listening and awareness

Thus there is inherent and necessary wisdom in the levels of attention that we give to the stimuli that bombard us from nature, from technology, and from other human beings. For were we to give equal attention to all sources we would be totally incapable of functioning. To avoid this form of madness, and once we feel safe and accustomed to any new environment or event, we subconsciously select the incoming vibrations that are worth attention. To some of these vibrations we give a higher accolade when, by translating and relating their significance to previous knowledge and experience, we pass their message into the realm of understanding.

Yet it is fascinating how even an elementary change in a usually safe situation can awaken our consciousness to a difference, even if there is that slight delay in recognition of the cause. Many of us have experienced that invisible alert when, for example, there is a change in the customary vibrations in a room. So, if even the stopping of a clock that usualy ticks can be noticeable, how much more do we somewhere notice those infinitesimal changes that are constantly emanating from other people's words through their voices?

Thus, while there are some sounds so compelling that we cannot, humanly, shut them off, we do shut off a myriad of others. As the eye is directed by lighting in the theatre, so our brain is the director of the process known as selective listening. And just as our manner of speaking reflects who we are and what we are like, so does our manner of listening, but much less obviously. This is perhaps one of the reasons why it is largely through what we say that we find out how we respond to life. Speaking and listening cannot be separated; like muscles, they go in pairs, their twin action reflecting the two sides of communication.

Listening, thinking, and responding

Since hearing is ever with us as a constant watchdog in our lives, it can be helpful to look into the process of paying attention, which elevates it to the level of listening; and particularly to the speed of listening, which is naturally pegged to that of speaking.

As we know from Chapter 7, on the preparation involved in giving a speech, the average rate of delivery is estimated at 125 words per minute (wpm). The average rate of thinking is estimated to be about three, and in some cases four, times faster. Here it is worth mentioning that it is considered that most people can hold a thought for approximately five seconds, with an average of five words, and occasionally whole phrases, retained in our memory bank prior to delivery. So when thinking while listening – or speaking – we are dealing with a fleeting activity and one which, by its very temporality apart from any other demands, can require total concentration. It is as if we have time for three thinking tracks when we are listening: one attending to what is being said; one feeding this and past trains of thought into memory; and one thinking ahead. A sign of effective communication comes when, during this last track, we begin to anticipate what the speaker is going to say, and even how he will conclude, just before, or as, he actually voices his thoughts aloud.

If the speaker is dull or repetitive, it can be hard for the listener to maintain the effort to think along with him. Among other reasons, there can seem little suspense or challenge in guessing his probable conclusions, especially if they are delivered through the sound of a familiar drone. So then we tend to listen intermittently, checking back on one of our tracks occasionally, while usually giving greater attention to matters elsewhere, thus absenting ourselves mentally from the scene.

Here, within our total context of use of the spoken word, it can be helpful to refer back to the speaker again, since it may now become evident why his role takes such a high degree of initiating energy and concentration. For, as you will realize, the effective speaker is likewise using those thinking tracks to maintain the thread of what he is saying, what he has said, and what he is about to say while keeping open to listener response.

While a few speakers can appear impervious to listener response, most will acknowledge how much they depend on a listener for the feedback of encouragement or need of clarification. This is one of the reasons why it is hard to practise any form of speaking in public while actually on our own. But the experience, hopefully rare, of talking to people who seem not to be giving the attention we feel we deserve can be unnerving, since they do not appear to be living up to our usual hopes and expectations. These tend to colour our attitude towards an event, and so the lack of response can distract by putting us off balance. This can lead to a break in those vital thinking tracks and create a potential for confidence to melt and, at awful worst, as Hamlet might continue, even thaw and resolve itself into a dew.

While such an unhappy thought is an extreme example, it is easy to take for granted the mystique that – except when on radio or at a public meeting, when gaining a microphone is essential to some people – he who is speaking calls the tune and is always in command of a situation. It is not often appreciated that while speaking and listening are interdependent, the listener can do much to make the work of the speaker successful. The signals he gives, unless he is editing his response with particular care, usually mirror his attitude and reception. The signals could be said to fall into approximately seven types, each ranging from positive to negative responses:

- Eye-contact, to eye wandering, and no contact;

- Leaning forward in stillness, to leaning back in listlessness;
- Smiling and nodding affirmatively, to yawning and shaking the head negatively;
- Catching another's eye with a look of agreement, to catching it with a grimace;
- Note-taking used discriminately, to note-taking showing only the top of the head;
- A look of acceptance, to a look of rejection and threat;
- Complete concentration, to partial or total concentration elsewhere, possibly leading to a different activity.

Whatever the usual listener response, however, it is interesting to note that every speaker also bears the task of being his own, everlasting listener; not in a narcissistic sense – although in most there is some gravitational pull towards the sound of their own voice – but to evaluate, and to remember, both the how and the what of the message. There is also the factor that everyone needs to hear what he is saying at the moment it is being said in order to keep his thoughts on track. Any chance of talking into a tape-recorder with a delayed-action response will give evidence of this. Equipped with ear-phones, the recorder creates a five-second delay before feeding the voice back to the speaker. The result can be temporarily disorientating as the speaker suddenly plods through an eerie vacuum of silence, followed by the odd impression of a delayed echo when the sound does come through. It soon appears that under such circumstances a unique concentration is required even to continue to think, and speak, ahead – let alone with some control of sound and approximation of sense.

Factors involved in listening

Having discussed hearing in general, we can now turn to the more particular factors involved in listening. One of the first things the reader might like to do is to review, from the listener's viewpoint, the introductory chapter on the human resources of communication. Just as we speak to inform, instruct, persuade, and entertain, so do we listen with similar purpose.

A large part of the effectiveness of listening rests on the twin acts of comprehension and memory. These in turn are then used for the essential activity of the correlation of ideas, which leads to understanding. So memory has a vital influence on the effectiveness of listening, and it is helpful to use it with care for the retention of key words. This private form of concentration requires an instant search for the precedence between major and minor points, and the maintenance of a periodic review similar to the cybernetic development of the house that Jack built. The 'Bingo!' of agreement occurs when the conclusions of listener and speaker coincide, but the wise man waits for the conclusion before attempting a full evaluation.

At the other end of the scale, it is best to avoid making assumptions, for these can carry an often unconscious burden of prejudice. This, in turn, like an attitude out of touch with reality, can lead to a closing, rather than opening, of minds. Added to which, it is valuable to aim to listen as openly as possible to everyone, since learning another's viewpoint gives a useful opportunity to join gaps in knowledge or to bridge differences of opinion.

Another means of closing such gaps is the diplomatic ability to elicit further information by questioning, which is an area we have already covered in an initiating sense in other chapters, and which is crucial to effective communication on any continuing basis. Choice of words, manner, and timing and the possible need to probe, as the listener temporarily becomes the speaker-listener, are interdependent. For example, the comment 'You've lost me' may be a clear signal of listener attitude, but it is unlikely to attract the speaker's co-operation. 'Could you clarify the point about –' is more likely to gain a useful response. Such an approach also gives a dual advantage for, by turning points of difficulty into questions, the listener can attempt to clarify his own thinking. Furthermore, he is pinpointing a gap in either the sending or receiving of information which, within reason, it is the speaker's responsibility to narrow.

An instance of such interchange comes from *Office Hours: Day and Night*, the autobiography of Dr Janet Travell, who was physician to President Kennedy. After once giving a public demonstration on the sources of pain, she commented, 'The hours that I spent with strangers who visited our booths were invaluable to me. I cannot measure how much I learned about two-way communication between people. My approach was to discover quickly what pegs of knowledge the enquirer had in his mind so that I could hang my facts on them. I had less difficulty in trying to rearrange his prejudices when what I offered sounded, not new, but vaguely familiar to my listener.' Her remarks also give a practical example of a useful dictum in all communication, that 'we learn by parallels of what we know.'

To listen with wisdom and discernment is a vital aspect of our communicating lives. It includes the need to deal with various distractions, which may range from red herrings to jargon, or from the introduction of irrelevant material to the weaponry of spurious emotional overtones and occasional verbal or vocal innuendo. Should such distractions be used, it is better either to ignore them, or to state them for what they are; though, like the handling of ignorance, their treatment often has to be tempered with careful use of energy in the service of diplomacy. At all costs, however, avoid becoming embattled in the same game, as a sense of proportion and objectivity are helpful in giving perspective to what is often a different value system.

But in the long run of life, listening largely depends on the relationships involved. These colour our purpose and the degree and span of attention we give, and they are in turn nearly always linked with the checks and balances of any pecking order involved at home, work, or play.

Listening and living

There is another aspect to listening which can be vital to well-being throughout our lives, and this is the apparently informal but vital communion that acts as a sounding board to human experience. For nothing helps us to perceive reality like encompassing it with our own spoken word. To some people and under some circumstances this can be done through the written word, but most of us need to voice our comprehension of an event. So to 'lend an ear' is not a mere hackneyed saying, but supplies one of the greatest needs of people facing the many degrees of loneliness. To be listened to, in the sense of being given time and responsive attention, is equally as important for the pensioner as for the toddler.

Yet if ever there was a stage in life where to be listened to responsively is vital, it is surely in childhood. Paying the respect of listening to young people is also tantamount to building a climate within which they can experiment with the voicing of emotion and thought through words; at the same time they can learn in turn to be a valuable listener to others later. Many people thinking back to their own childhood have cause to be grateful to an adult, not necessarily in the family, who often gave personal interest and consideration in this way. Being able to discuss matters and converse with someone from another age level usually brings out the best in a person, and it hinges not only on liking but on being heard with attention and understanding.

The teenager also experiences a time when to hear himself articulate some of the challenges of his age-group is invaluable. That this need does not disappear later in life is put with driving simplicity by the wife of the exhausted Willy Loman in Arthur Miller's *Death of a Salesman*. At a time when his personal crisis is being lost in a family vortex she claims, 'Attention must finally be paid to such a person.'

It is now an established practice in psychiatry that much therapy can be accomplished by the client outering a whole spectrum of his experiences. Initially these may be fractured, and yet gradually as utterance leads to acceptance and health becomes whole, we have another reminder of the use of good words. Yet how much greater use might be made if, along the emotional parameters of life, more people were available to listen. Most, at any age, value a talking out of experience, whether to share wonder and joy, or to make some sense of despair and grief. To meet this need, many associations have been formed, ranging from crisis centres to deal with extreme needs, to Alcoholics Anonymous, to associations for those recently widowed, or for those who find themselves single parents.

Meanwhile the spoken word continues as the cornerstone of all the ritual of our lives, pronouncing our names at birth, at marriage, and at the experience we call death; passing back into the air those little exhalations that, in all time, signal only and for ever, the needs, hopes, fears, and joys that are just us.

Voice routine

Continue to develop your routine from preparation into exercises, and then into their application in different kinds of verse, before doing some reading aloud. As you widen your selection, try to choose material in which the content is inherently well expressed whether in terms of a serious or a lighter mood. Good speaking-prose, for example, will give you the sense of the architecture of a sentence; remember those balanced phrases at the beginning of the passage suggested for your control tape, 'It was the best of times, it was the worst of times ...'? For the more you breathe voice into good structure, the more your ear will carry echoes and an appreciation of standards; not for mimicry, but for yardsticks against which your own development can grow.

It goes without saying that all exercises, every conversation you have, every class or social or business function you attend, is as concerned with listening as with speaking. And whether a text such as this should begin or end with the topic is like the argument about the chicken and the egg. So last, but infinitely not least, are some brief assignments in different aspects of listening.

Assignments

AWARENESS
– Take a rhythm, such as various kinds of clapping, and pass it on round the group. As everyone becomes reliable, use more complex rhythms.
– Return to a simple rhythm, but ask every fourth or sixth person to develop a variation of it, while keeping to the same beat.

- Later aim for more variations with more complex rhythms.
- Take a sound and pass it on. This can include various categories such as nature sounds, animal sounds, and machine sounds. After a few rounds, explore and improvise within a category: a pair of machines develops into the sounds of a factory floor, or a wind into a storm at sea and back to calm.
- To explore the beginnings of more human sounds, try the tunes involved in a conversation just by whistling; or use the varying lengths and curls of a humming sound.

DIRECTIONS
- Assume your partner is out walking, cycling, or driving and is lost. Prepare four or five directions: 'Go back half a mile. Turn left at the school, right at the police station, and it's the second on the left.' As people often do before moving on, your partner repeats the directions. Then change roles.
- Extend to include complications and landmarks such as street and place names, bus routes, or bridges, hills, and rivers.

ERRANDS AND MESSAGES
- You are about to go shopping when your partner calls out a list of extras. Repeat, as before.
- Over a few weeks extend the list, and later see if you can retain it for a repeat at the end of the class or session.
- Give orders as to a waiter or waitress; as for an office lunch or party; as for an assistant to a plumber or carpenter, or to a technician or handyman. Ask him or her to repeat your order correctly.

Remember that visualization and association play an important part in recall, so as you begin to memorize an item, try to see it within the pattern of some context, so that one aspect automatically reminds you of the next.

DESCRIPTION
- Ask your partner to fold a piece of paper in certain ways. Change roles.
- Describe a diagram you have in front of you; your partner draws it without seeing it. Change roles.
- You are working in an office. Your partner phones in to ask you to bring items to a meeting and describes where you will find them; they include files, lists, notes, and books. Go through the motions. When successfully completed, change roles.

ORAL PRECIS
- Your partner tells a three- or four-minute anecdote. Give a one-minute precis reproducing the major order of events.
- Whisper a brief anecdote or message round a group. Note if it has changed as the last person repeats it.

NOTE-TAKING
Accurate listening, which involves the ability to be aware of key words, is important in taking notes, which should not become overlong and involved.

- When someone is giving an oral report or speech to your group, use the opportunity to make clear notes. Keep them simple, and try to record the main order of headings and sub-headings. Later compare notes with the speaker to see if there is a resemblance in the main outline.

AN INTERVIEWING PROJECT

Outline
Here is an assignment that can provide a valuable learning experience for speakers and listeners, and is an expansion of previous ideas about going out into the community. It involves each member of a group interviewing people in different occupations, and afterwards giving an oral report.

The assignment could focus on one topic such as speech in the community; it could then involve finding out what part this form of communication plays in the working lives of people in many occupations. So people to be interviewed might include a lawyer, waitress, policeman, social worker, sales-person, bank manager, repairman, or executive.

Or members could focus on one topic in order to learn about the daily workings of a large organization. Contact, and then arrangements, might be made with the administrator of an airport, hospital, or hotel, or with the manager of a newspaper or radio or television station. Or, again through request, members might look into the whole process and the many details involved in preparing the arts for public presentation. This could include meeting those putting on a play, ballet, or opera; preparing a concert or an exhibit at a gallery, museum, or library; or preparing a film or a television production. Other ideas might cover the making and marketing of local products, or finding out about the design of a new shopping centre, or of street furniture, or about the publication of a book.

Again, topics can be as wide as the universe, and can be adapted to specific subjects so that the assignment virtually becomes a form of oral documentary on various authors in literature, or on events as viewed through the people involved in history, or on developments in science.

The report
Each report should be taped during delivery and should last a previously agreed time of between five and ten minutes. It may be spoken from notes, but not written out and read aloud. The aim is to synthesize the experience of meeting the people involved, and to convey the atmosphere of their surroundings, and the facts, as accurately as possible in the time available.

The assessment
The assessment involves active participation, with four members and the teacher or leader filling in a form a few minutes after each report. Four major headings make a useful start, including: content and whether it kept to the topic; organization; delivery; and any general comment. Remarks should be constructive. Any need to project, or a tendency to use 'er' and 'um,' is usually noticed by everyone. The teacher may like to glance through the comments and give them, with his own, to the respective speakers at the next session; or he might go through the comments personally if the speaker would like to hear the tape of his report.

Assessment can also be made orally following each speaker; either on a random basis, or with some people asked to note some aspects in advance. The major question is, did the speaker communicate?

Benefits
One or two comprehensive oral projects a year make a good balance to written work. They spread knowledge widely, rather than privately to the teacher, create a form of communal enthusiasm and interest, and, through their assessment, provide experience in comment without giving offence. Through occasional divergence of opinion, they can show students how to allow for and respect a different response to the same stimulus; and they provide opportunity to weigh the spoken word, as we constantly do the written word, in the balance of a receptive mind.

SUMMARY
The ability to summarize the spoken word requires an additional dimension to that required for oral precis of the written word. It is usually given in the presence of the people concerned, and with an appreciation of what they said and how they said it. They in turn can indicate acceptance or otherwise of the statements. Meanwhile, to summarize someone else's views in terms imme-

diately acceptable to them requires a tactful understanding of a situation, and fairness to everyone involved.

- In groups of four to six people, have a short but sometimes sharp final discussion about an issue on which everyone will shortly vote.
- For example, will members of a special committee recommend plans for a new civic centre or for a housing estate? Prior to the vote the chairman summarizes each person's position.
- Should the discussion become heated, the chairman may, as an aid to understanding, invite each member to summarize the views of the previous speaker before proceeding to the next point themselves.

DISCERNMENT

Many assignments designed to help listening are concerned with the factual aspects of comprehension and memory. But as noted in Chapter 4, our ability to use the spoken word evolves out of not one but two systems: the intuitive sound of voice linked with the acquired habit of speech, which together become the servant of language.

Thus an important aspect of listening is to become aware of the twin tracks of sound and meaning, which usually complement each other. But occasionally we get hints that they diverge and this is where discernment, as sometimes in summarizing, is needed. Is it that the speaker senses the meaning, but is at a loss for words? Or does he have the words but is unable to express the feeling? Or is he being diplomatic, or controlling feeling, evading an issue, withholding information, or using vocal threats or verbal weapons? Or if he speaks with an accent that may be linguistic or national, is he inadvertently imposing the vocal signals and values of one culture on another?

Wisdom can be needed in sizing up the person and/or their role within a situation, and in deciding whether we should listen primarily to their vocal or their verbal message; often the former, being part of a more primitive mechanism, is the more reliable gauge. Perhaps among those who could tell us most about these less measurable aspects of listening are the long-experienced psychologists we call playwrights and actors, who surely hold not just a mirror up to nature, but also open our ears to it. And it has been noted that those lower in the scale of any pecking order of this world have a special awareness of the balance between the signals they receive.

It is useful to become aware of the unspoken dialogue that we hear and use throughout our lives. To help you do so, it is time to become your own playwright in residence again. With a partner, and remembering to develop a sub-text, try:

- A politician being interviewed by a reporter on radio or television news.
- A delegate at a UN reception being suave to his enemy.
- A boss having to tell an employee to take an early retirement.
- Change roles; develop your own situations.
- Re-read the lines of a play, and note the unspoken implications of the sub-text.

In drama, as in life, remember there are countless times when what is not said can, for a number of reasons, be more important that what is said; and the clue usually lies in monitoring the 'how.'

And then there are times when whole echoes of meaning and memory may be evoked by the complementary sounds of a limited number of words, as in this scene from *David Copperfield* in which two men are watching a woman tend her dying husband.

'He's a-going out with the tide,' said Mr Pegotty to me, behind his hand.
My eyes were dim, and so were Mr Pegotty's, but I repeated in a whisper,
'With the tide?'
'People can't die along the coast,' said Mr Pegotty, 'except when the tide's pretty nigh out. They can't be born, unless it's pretty nigh in – not properly born, till flood.'   From *David Copperfield*, Charles Dickens

P.S.

So there you have it. You have made a beginning. Continue by reading books on the topic that look interesting, and often those that are not too long and avoid jargon are the most helpful. But obviously it is best to balance any such background by work with a good teacher. We are, after all, dealing with an essentially practical subject, and few of us would try to study the motions of a sport or of singing or dancing solely from a book. Teaching that will stand the test of usefulness over a period of time depends not just on a 'do this' and 'do that' scheme of things, but on the personal application and constant checking of effective principles. In the case of speech, these stem from the sciences, including anatomy, physiology, physics, and phonetics. They can then be linked to the disciplines of communication required in the arts involved, whether concerned with public speaking or verse speaking, or with theatre or debate.

Among areas we may not appear to have touched on directly is what to do about first aid for poor voices or untidy speech. Initially, if suddenly faced with the need to speak in public, people may think that, if someone pin-points what could be labelled 'wrong,' all they need is a few tips and away they go. Sometimes, if they have a good ear, are willing and well co-ordinated, such tips can suffice; but because of the interrelationship of the factors involved, it is often more complicated than that. The best approach is usually to start, not with what is wrong, but with the assumption that much is right, and to progress with a positive attitude from there.

For example, most of us are born with a more than expressive voice and the physical ability to articulate clearly. It is what we do with the mechanism later that counts. By starting at square one, as in our early exercises and voice routine, we are unwinding any habits of prevention, but always establishing a way to effective use. Then, if it is possible to continue with a course that gives positive experience in all manner of communication through speech, we are the better prepared to use this marvellous facility throughout life.

We all know, however, that while you can lead a horse to water, you cannot always get it to do the other thing, and there are times when people are hesitant to move out of a vocal or verbal rut. It can seem unreasonable to try to impose standards that may appear artificial, and that sound and feel strange, on someone who grunts among the mumbles of sloppy speech. But by a sense of communal development in a group or class, it is possible to offer a workable alternative. Once one or two members produce evidence of improved communication during the practice of assignments and their application to other situations, often including the working world, it can be interesting to note the spin-off on others.

All of which brings us back to the reminder that speech is an imitative affair; and once we have gone beyond the initial influence of the tribe, and sometimes of teachers generally, we can still be subject to that of other spheres. These can change during our lives as they do during history, and while voice recordings can take us back about a hundred years, we can otherwise only surmise about fashions in speech from the dialogue of novels and plays. Sounds can run their course of substitution as in the 'wim, wigour and witality' of Dickens' time, or the exchange of w's for r's in the effusive 'Wather!' of some late Victorians; or they may be omitted as in the one-time jet-set's 'huntin' and shootin'.' There was even a time when so-called gentility was suggested by the hesitancy of a slightly affected stammer, perhaps so as to avoid coming on too strong.

We tend to keep up with our times by adapting the vocal as well as the verbal idiom. Until recently, the fashions were usually set by those who talked what was thought proper, as assimilated through tribe and school. Now some of the advantages of universal education are occasionally offset by an opposite trend, with an influence arising from a democratic sense of keeping company with the less articulate.

There is also a tendency creeping in through the media on both sides of the Atlantic to use emphasis in a way that seems to negate meaning. A voice-over on a commercial may claim that Brand X *is* the best, or expound the benefits *of* a new car, or tell you to come *to* a new shopping area. It is a wonder that sponsors do not listen more carefully, for if we heard in real life that something '*is*' so vehemently, it could signal rebuttal of a previous statement, and so even raise doubts about a product. In the usual course of things we might simply want to remember its name, and the fact that it is the best.

Such, hopefully unintentional, mis-emphasis is also noticeable on the part of some, but not the major, newsreaders on radio and television, who may announce that Mr So-and-so has just come *from* London, or Ottawa or New York (surely nobody said he has not?) or that he will shortly be going *to* Australia. Presumably we need to be informed about his destination, rather than to receive a plug about the direction of his going.

This pattern of 'mediaese' can also occur in some interviews, where the guest may fall into a similar style. This is unfortunate in not only creating some barrier to meaning, but in giving an artificiality to the occasion. It would rarely be a true extension of how someone usually speaks, but may be part of a subconscious feeling that additional effort must be made to be on some kind of best behaviour.

Meanwhile, during introductory classes in speech communication someone invariably asks, 'Who would you suggest as an example of a really good speaker?' – and then sits back while everybody relaxes. This usually comes when initial exercises are over, trial runs at breathing and projection have been made, and the heat is temporarily elsewhere. The query seems that bit removed from what we have been doing or talking about. Illustrious names swim through the room; maybe a Dylan Thomas will be cited as a reader, a Claire Bloom as an actress, or an Alistair Cooke as an apt dealer in words on the media.

The answer is simple but has a preface: Depending on the full development of potential – you. And everyone genuinely interested.

This book was typeset by

TITLE PAGE INC.

in 10 on 12 Times Roman
with headings in 18 pt Helvetica Bold
Diagrams are by Acorn Technical Art and
the book was printed and bound by
University of Toronto Press